Carnegie Hall New York

Music Festival under the Direction of Walter Damrosch

Carnegie Hall New York

Music Festival under the Direction of Walter Damrosch

ISBN/EAN: 9783337811730

Printed in Europe, USA, Canada, Australia, Japan

Cover: Foto ©Thomas Meinert / pixelio.de

More available books at **www.hansebooks.com**

Music Fest...

●●●

Under the Direction of

WALTER DAMROSCH

●●●

FOR THE INAUGURATION OF

'MUSIC HALL"

FOUNDED BY ANDREW CARNEGIE.

5th, 6th, 7th, 8th, 9th, 1891.

UNDER THE DIRECTION OF

WALTER DAMROSCH

...URATION OF

HALL"

...W CARNEGIE

8TH AND 9TH, ...

...D PUBLISHING COMPANY

VANDEWATER STREET

ANDREW CARNEGIE

MUSIC HALL COMPANY OF NEW YORK,

LIMITED.

BOARD OF DIRECTORS.

MORRIS RENO,	- - -	PRESIDENT.
STEPHEN M. KNEVALS, -	- -	TREASURER.
FREDERICK WM. HOLLS,	- -	SECRETARY.

JOHN W. AITKEN.   ANDREW CARNEGIE.

WALTER DAMROSCH.   WILLIAM S. HAWK.

SHERMAN W. KNEVALS.   WILLIAM B. TUTHILL.

EXECUTIVE COMMITTEE.

MORRIS RENO.   STEPHEN M. KNEVALS.

FREDERICK WM. HOLLS.   WALTER DAMROSCH.

WILLIAM S. HAWK.

Office : MUSIC HALL, 57TH STREET AND 7TH AVENUE.

CONTENTS.

❖

LIST OF WORKS

TO BE PERFORMED AT THE FESTIVAL

First Concert.

Tuesday Evening, May 5th.

"OLD HUNDRED."

ORATION: *Dedication of the Hall* -   - RT. REV. HENRY C. POTTER, D.D.

NATIONAL HYMN, *"America."*

OVERTURE, *Leonore No. III*   -   -   -   -   -   -   -   BEETHOVEN

MARCHE SOLENNELLE   -   -   -   -   -   -   -   TSCHAIKOWSKY

TE DEUM   -   -   -   -   -   -   -   -   -   -   -   BERLIOZ
(First time in New York.)   For Tenor Solo, Triple Chorus and Orchestra.

Second Concert.

Wednesday Evening, May 6th.

ELIJAH, Oratorio for Soli, Chorus and Orchestra   -   -   MENDELSSOHN

Third Concert.

Thursday Afternoon, May 7th.

OVERTURE to *Figaro*   -   -   -   -   -   -   -   -   -   MOZART

GRAND FINALE, Act II., *Figaro*   -   -   -   -   MOZART

SUITE No. III., for Orchestra   -   -   -   -   -   TSCHAIKOWSKY

SUITE No. III., Op. 55, -   -   -   -   -   TSCHAIKOWSKY

ARIA from *L'Esclarmonde*   -   -   -   -   -   -   MASSENET

ARIA from *Le Roi de Lahore* -   -   -   -   -   -   MASSENET

PRELUDE AND FINALE from *Tristan and Isolde*   -   -   -   WAGNER

Fourth Concert.

Friday Evening, May 8th.

THE SEVEN WORDS OF OUR SAVIOUR -   -   HEINRICH SCHUETZ
(Seventeenth Century.) (First time in America.)
For Soli, Chorus, String Orchestra and Organ.

TWO A CAPELLA CHORUSES: ⎱
  a. PATER NOSTER.   ⎰ -   -   -   -   -   TSCHAIKOWSKY
  b. LEGEND.
(New. First time in America.)

SULAMITH -   -   -   -   -   -   -   -   LEOPOLD DAMROSCH
For Soli, Chorus and Orchestra.

Fifth Concert.

Saturday Afternoon, May 9th.

FIFTH SYMPHONY, C Minor -   -   -   -   -   BEETHOVEN

SONGS { " *To Sleep* " (Tennyson) -   -   -   WALTER DAMROSCH
       { " *So Schmerzlich* " -   -   -   -   TSCHAIKOWSKY

CONCERTO for Piano with Orchestra. B flat minor, Op. 23, TSCHAIKOWSKY
  I. Andante non troppo e molto maestoso. Allegro con spirito.
  II. Andantino simplice.   III. Allegro con fuoco.

PRELUDE,   ⎱ FROM *Parsifal* -   -   -   WAGNER
FLOWER MAIDEN SCENE, Act II. ⎰
For Six Solo Voices and Female Chorus.

Sixth Concert.

Saturday Evening, May 9th.

ISRAEL IN EGYPT, Oratorio -   -   -   -   -   -   -   HANDEL
For Soli, Double Chorus and Orchestra.

INTRODUCTION.

✿ ✿ ✿

LEVEN YEARS AGO, on May 3, 4, 5, 6 and 7, 1881, Dr. Leopold Damrosch gave, with the assistance of the Oratorio Society, the Symphony Society and an increased chorus, his first Musical Festival, in the Seventh Regiment Armory. After that time, up to the present, the two societies had no place in which their efforts could be brought to the highest artistic results. They went first to the Academy of Music, and later to the Metropolitan Opera House, but neither of these places proved satisfactory for concert purposes or for the production of great choral works.

At last, however, to-day, the two societies, homeless so long, are able to hold a festival that marks a distinct period in the musical history of New York. At last the great metropolis is able to rejoice in the possession of a temple of Music, which, it is intended, shall be a home not only for the Oratorio and Symphony Societies, but for all musical societies and organizations whose aim is the cultivation of the highest class of music. It is a temple, solid as granite without, made lovely within, a wonderful home for the most beautiful of the arts, the gift of one who has made the advancement of humanity in Literature, Art, Science and Music on both sides of the Atlantic the glory of a busy and successful life. Mr. Andrew Carnegie has expressed to the world his conviction that the man who dies rich without having allotted during his lifetime a portion of his share of the world's goods for the benefit of mankind ends a life disgraced ; and MUSIC HALL is only one of a long series of munificent gifts from which the peoples of two countries will gain untold good, now and in the future.

At the Festival of 1881 the large choral works produced were Handel's *Dettingen Te Deum*, Rubinstein's sacred opera, *The Tower of Babel*, Berlioz' *Grande Messe des Morts*, *Requiem*, Handel's *Messiah*, two of Beethoven's symphonies, the Fifth and the Ninth, and excerpts from several of Wagner's music-dramas. The great choral works of the Festival were religious in character. It was always Dr. Damrosch's endeavor to show as an incontestable truth that in the whole course of musical development the religious spirit has inspired the greatest compositions. The works selected, therefore, were all more or less intimately connected with the outgrowth of the religious influence in music, and they were placed on the evening programmes in order that the evening concerts should have a consistent purpose, and also that all the members of the chorus might assist in their performance. The same elevated aim is, it will be seen, to be maintained through the present series of concerts.

The Festival will be essentially a choral one. It has been the aim of the conductor to make the programmes sufficiently varied, and to represent various developments of choral writing, from the old and quaintly beautiful *Seven Words*, by Schütz, who in that work gave to the world the first German Passion-oratorio that was ever written, through the oratorios of Handel, whose *Israel in Egypt* was his greatest choral work, to his more modern follower, Mendelssohn, whose masterpiece *Elijah* will be heard, and down to the modern development of the religious cantata, in Leopold Damrosch's *Sulamith*.

The work of Schütz (1585—1672) marks the second period in the evolution of the Oratorio, when the ancient music to the Mysteries and Passion-plays was released from the religious stage, and began the course that finally led to Bach and Handel. In the *Seven Words* and in the same composer's *Die Auferstehung Christi* are found the germs of the modern oratorio. It was Schütz' mission to bring the earlier Passion-music into oratorio form, which Bach took further forward in his Passion-oratorios, and to which Handel gave heroic proportions.

It is peculiarly fitting that Dr. Leopold Damrosch's *Sulamith* should be given at the present Festival. Its performance by the members of the Oratorio Society and the orchestra of the Symphony Society, under the baton of the composer's son, will naturally assume

x

the character of an *"In Memoriam"* of one without whose noble efforts to achieve the highest position in the American musical world the present Festival would not have been possible. Dr. Damrosch was the founder of the Oratorio Society, and his *Sulamith* was written for and produced by that body for the first time in April, 1882. It was therefore eminently fitting that a place should be given on the Festival programme of to-day to the work of one who always looked forward with confidence to the time when music should have a home of its own in New York, though he himself did not live to see his hopes realized.

The desire of the conductor of the Festival has, further, been to make the programmes of the Festival as thoroughly catholic in character as possible, so as to embrace all the schools in music ; also to test the acoustic properties of the hall through the different styles of musical expression, from the simple song to the great oratorios demanding immense choruses, and to the passionate orchestration of Richard Wagner. Berlioz, who has been recognized as the Wagner of France, will be heard in his best work, the *Te Deum*, which gives a magnificent example of fine choral and contrapuntal writing and of the brilliant instrumentation so characteristic of the French composer. To Dr. Leopold Damrosch belongs the honor of having made American audiences better acquainted with Berlioz. He it was who produced first in this country the French composer's *Symphonie Fantastique*, his *Romeo and Juliet* overture, his *Harold* symphony, his *Damnation of Faust ;* and his *Grand Messe des Morts, Requiem,* was a feature of the Festival of 1881.

The selection of the great *Finale* from the second act of *The Marriage of Figaro* will reveal Mozart in his most charming mood. The delightful septet is one of the gems of a work that is justly considered the best of all musical comedies, and to many people it will come with almost the charm of novelty. Wagner will be represented by two of his most characteristic works, in selections from *Tristan and Isolde* and the Prelude and Flower Maiden scene from his *Parsifal ;* while to Beethoven is accorded, with his *Leonore* Overture No. 3, the first number on the programme, and with it MUSIC HALL will receive its public baptism of music.

The engagement of the Russian composer Tschaikowsky adds a very pleasant and original feature to the Festival. He is the greatest representative Russian composer living to-day, sharing with Brahms and Saint-Saens the honors of European fame. He will be heard in several of his own best creations, among them a march, two *a capella* choruses written in the style of Palestrina and Orlando di Lasso, his Suite No. 3 for orchestra, and his Concerto No. 1 for piano and orchestra. M. Tschaikowsky will also take a prominent part in the Festival, in conducting his own compositions. It will be the first time in America's musical history that a Russian composer will wield the baton. No country in Europe, it may be added, has made such remarkable advance in music as Russia has during the last three or four decades. The seed-thought of national music sown by Wagner in Germany has apparently taken permanent root in the great empire, and, with the traditional splendor of the music of the Greek church and the folk-songs of the people, has developed wonderful blossoms.

Most of the singers who will be heard at the Festival are so well known from their artistic work in connection with the recent seasons of opera and concert that any extended record of their careers seems to be superfluous. Signor Campanini is still the representative Italian tenor among us. Frau Antonia Mielke, Frau Marie Ritter-Goetze, Herrn Emil Fischer, Theodor Reichmann, Andreas Dippel and Conrad Behrens were the main supports of the recent season of grand opera in German at the Metropolitan. Mlle. Clementine de Vere, Mrs. Theodore J. Toedt, Mrs. Carl Alves, Mrs. Gerrit Smith, Miss Anna Luella Kelly, Mrs. Hattie Clapper-Morris and Mr. Ericson Bushnell complete the list of singers. The pianiste of the Festival is Frl. Aus der Ohe, who has endeared herself to the American public through five seasons of successful artistic work.

The • Music • Festival.

OVERTURE.

LEONORE No. 3, - BEETHOVEN.

"NOTHING can be more sublime than to draw nearer to the Godhead than other men, and to diffuse here on earth these godlike rays among mortals.   *   * I willingly renounce the world which has no presentiment that Music is a higher revelation than all their wisdom and philosophy."—BEETHOVEN.

" How the poems of antiquity, though so beautiful and so admired, pale before this marvel of modern music ! Theocritus and Virgil were great landscape songsters. Their verses are soft music, but Beethoven's tone-poems ! Ye poor great poets of antiquity, ye poor immortals, veil your faces ; your conventional language, so pure, so harmonious, cannot vie with the art of Sounds. Ye are glorious, but conquered ! Ye have not known what we to-day call melody, harmony, the combinations of varying timbres, instrumental coloring, modulations, the learned conflicts of sounds, which war first and afterwards kiss, those surprises which move our souls to their very depths. The stammerings of an art in its infancy, which you called music, could not give you any idea of all this ; for the eminent and cultured minds of your age, you were the great melodists, the harmonists, the masters of rhythm and expression. But these words in your language had a very different meaning from that which we give them to-day. The art of Sounds, strictly speaking, is born but of yesterday ; it is hardly an adult ; it is beautiful, it is all-powerful ; it is the Pythian Apollo of the moderns. We owe it a world of sentiments and sensations, which for you was unrevealed. Ye great poets, whom we worship, ye are conquered !"—BERLIOZ.

TSCHAIKOWSKY.

MARCH SOLENELLE.

Conducted by the Composer.

IN a review of Russian music published in a London musical journal a short time ago occurs the following sentence :—" The progress which Russia is making in musical art is being watched with interest by all musicians. The St. Petersburg Conservatorium, founded by Rubinstein in 1862, has produced at least one composer of note, Peter Tschaikowsky, whose songs and pianoforte pieces are known throughout Europe." Not long before, Liszt made a remark to Janka Wohl, which she records in her " Recollections of Liszt," as follows :—" Properly speaking, there is as yet no Russian music, but there are some first-rate composers. The Russian mind, which is in continual activity on the one side, and comatose on the other, will have to do an immense amount of work in order to properly direct its natural tendencies ; and this is the result of the climate of the country and of the Sclav character in general. . . . One feels that the Russian composers go to work under a more or less sentimental inspiration, and not under the all-powerful impression of a master idea."

American audiences have had ample opportunity, however, in the last decade, to estimate for themselves the merits and demerits of the Russian school of music, and the judgment expressed upon it has been of profound admiration for its originality, strength, color and beauty. The performance in New York of Tschaikowsky's Symphony after Bryon's Manfred, five years ago, induced a well-known writer to say :—" Tschaikowsky's symphony provided an agreeable surprise. It is a highly imaginative and beautiful work, quite as remarkable for the deep, poetical feeling pervading it as for the ingenuity of its instrumentation, which would not be shamed by the best efforts of Berlioz. It would not be altogether fanciful if one should cite a dozen or so compositions of the young Russian school as arguments that the musical scepter which the Teutons have wielded for so long is in danger of passing into Sclavic hands. Such daring and vigor as some of Tschaikowsky's music, including this new symphony, displays, without impairment of these qualities by obvious harmonical and other theoretical subtleties, mean something to the student of musical history. Look out for the Muscovite. He's a dangerous power in politics, and the musical supremacy of Germany is being threatened." Robert Hamerling, the Austrian poet, exclaims in his poem of " Die sieben Todsuenden":—

> " Up to the conflict, ye Romans and Germans,
> We're the Colossus, and dwarfs are ye !
> With us henceforth rests the fate of Europa,
> Lord of the world soon the Sclav must be !"

The names of Russian composers are now familiar features on nearly all the programmes of our great concert leaders. Russian music is not an artificial growth, or the product of a hot-house system of forcing, as is the case too often in countries where popular and national melodies have not taken root during centuries of history. The Greek Church has done quite as much as the Roman to keep music in the hearts of the Russian people, and Russian Czars have not neglected to give due attention to the furtherance of musical culture in the vast empire. The services of the church are entirely choral, no organ or instrument being permitted. The choirs in the cathedrals, composed of a large number of voices, are conducted with extraordinary precision and accuracy, and the voices are distinguished by great delicacy of tone and expression. A few years ago a celebrated Russian choir was heard in London and Paris, and M. Gounod said of their performances:—" No choir in these days presents such thorough homogeneity of execution." Some of the bass voices created astonishment for their beauty of tone, with a full body of sound, like the pedal pipes of an organ. Those who were permitted to be present at the Coronation of the present Czar at Moscow, in 1883, will remember with what surprise they listened to the marvelous voices of the male choir.

Without going into the history of Russian secular music, and its gradual release from foreign influences, it may be well to quote a few facts of interest:—At the beginning of the nineteenth century great attention began to be paid to instrumental music. In 1802 the Philharmonic Society was founded. In the realm of opera Italian composers occupied the field till the end of the second decade of the present century. A pupil of Field, Verstovskig, wrote several operas in the Russian tongue, and he is regarded as the first representative of modern Russian dramatic music. Next to him may be named Glinka, whose *Life for the Czar* was given in St. Petersburg in 1836, and was received with acclamation. He was a pupil of Field, and, after completing his studies in Italy and Germany, he became court conductor and director of the imperial opera. In 1863 a Russian composer named Serov produced a five act opera, *Judith*, in St. Petersburg, and attracted considerable attention ; the music was described as melodious and Sclavonic in character, while as to form Wagner seems to have been the composer's model.

The two foremost musicians of Russia to-day are Anton Rubinstein and Peter Tschaikowsky. Rubinstein's life belongs to the history of modern Russian music so intimately that the two cannot be separated. In 1859 he stood at the head of the Russian Musical Society, and in 1862 established the St. Petersburg Conservatorium, of which institution he was director until 1867. From that time till 1878 he made concert tours in Europe and America, and composed, until in 1887 he again took the direction of the St. Petersburg Conservatory. Of his many works his "Ocean" and "Dramatic" symphonies have made the round of the world. These, with his many operas, biblical dramas, his hundreds of compositions for the concert room, have given Russian music glory everywhere.

M. Tschaikowsky—Peter Iljitsch Tschaikowsky—is the author of several operas, five symphonies, several overtures, two pianoforte concertos, a violin concerto, three string quartets, besides a large number of vocal and instrumental works. He was born in 1840, in the Russian province of Wjatka, in the Urals, and, after having studied jurisprudence, occupied for a time a post as under secretary in the Ministry of Justice. His tastes, however, being altogether musical, he left the service of the state, and in 1862 entered the newly founded Conservatory, and after studying six years he gained the prize medal for a contata on Schiller's *Ode to Joy*. From 1866 to 1877 he was teacher of musical theory at the Moscow Conservatory. Since then he has devoted himself entirely to musical composition, living alternately in St. Petersburg, Italy or Switzerland. Among his works are his orchestral fantasies on "Manfred," on Shakespeare's "Tempest" and on "Francesca di Rimini," his overture to "Romeo and Juliet," and his operas *Voyvode*, *Opritschnik*, *Walkula*, which gained the prize of the Russian Music Society, *Eugen Onagin*, *Joan of Arc*, *Mazeppa*, *Pique Dame*, a lyric drama, *Snow White*, and a ballet, *The Lake of Swans*. He has fairly won his position as the greatest representative living Russian composer.

All of M. Tschaikowsky's best works have been heard in New York. In 1883 Dr. Leopold Damrosch gave the No. 2 Symphony at a concert of the Symphony Society. This work was repeated, under Mr. Walter Damrosch, in the season of 1888–1889, at one of the concerts of the Symphony Society, together with the Concerto for Violin. In the season of 1889–1890 Mr. Walter Damrosch gave the Symphony No. 4, at the fourth concert of the Symphony Society. The *Cappriccio Italien* has also been given by the Symphony Society, under the conductorship of Mr. Damrosch, who, like Mr. Theodore Thomas, has for some years past given the Russian composer a prominent place on his programmes. Besides the March Solenelle, M. Tschaikowsky will conduct his Suite No. 3 for orchestra, two *a capella* choruses, which will be heard for the first time in America, and his Concerto No. 1 for piano and orchestra. Descriptions of these works will be found on another page.

M. Tschaikowsky's musical proclivities have been summed up in Sir George Grove's great work as follows:—" In the works of a highly-educated musician like M. Tschaikowsky, it would be vain to look for anything narrowly national, specifically Russian. Though he does not dream of serving up the songs and dances of his country in all their rude and crude beauty, his music nevertheless bears the unmistakable impress of Slavonic temperament—fiery exaltation on the basis of languid melancholy. Like most Slavonic poets, Polish or Russian, he shows a predilection for huge and fantastic outlines, for subtleties of diction, and luxuriant growth of words and images, together with an almost oriental delight in gorgeous colors."

Te Deum

FOR THREE CHOIRS, ORCHESTRA AND ORGAN, Op. 22.

BERLIOZ.

1.	Triple Chorus,	-	- - -	"Te Deum laudamus."
2.	Triple Chorus,	-	- -	"Tibi omnes Angeli."
3.	Double Chorus,	-	- - -	"Dignare, Domine."
4.	Double Chorus,	-	- -	"Christe, Rex Gloriae."
5.	Tenor Solo and Double Chorus,	-		"Te ergo quaesumus."
6.	Triple Chorus,	-	- -	"Judex crederis."
7.	March,	-	- - - -	Pour la Presentation des Drapeaux.

HE genius of Hector Berlioz was recognized tardily by the world. To-day he is called the Wagner of France. His genius was first recognized by the Germans. The last words of his autobiography are: "I thank, from the bottom of my heart, holy Germany, where the religion of Art is kept unsullied, and thee generous England and thee Russia, who saved me, and you my good friends in France, and you all noble hearts and spirits of all countries whom I have known. To know you has been my joy, I will keep faithfully the dear remembrance of our friendship." Berlioz would probably have included America in his gratitude had he lived long enough, for nowhere has his genius been so readily acknowledged.

Born in 1803, dying in 1869, the present work dates from the period of his greatest musical activity. In 1840 he had written his *Symphonie Funebre et Triumphale.* In 1845 and 1846 he visited Germany. At Dresden he met the young Kapellmeister Richard Wagner, who helped him in rehearsals with zeal and good will. Mendelssohn he met at Leipsic. While at Berlin he wrote: "Music is in the air, you breathe it." There he heard Bach's music and gave two successful concerts, at which Meyerbeer assisted him. During a second concert tour in 1846 he composed his *Damnation of Faust,* the work produced for the first time in this country by Dr. Leopold Damrosch at Steinway Hall, eleven years ago. It was in 1849 that he wrote the present work.

Richard Pohl in his "*Hector Berlioz : Studien und Erinnerungen*" gives some facts of interest in connection with the first performance of the *Te Deum* in Germany. Berlioz, he says, was instigated to the composition of the *Te Deum* by the desire he entertained in 1849 of composing a grand epic-dramatical work on the largest possible scale, in representation and glorification of the military fame of Napoleon I., under the title of *The Return of the First Consul from his Italian Campaign.* In this prodigious work the *Te Deum* was to form only an episode. The idea was, Dr. Pohl continues, that at the moment of the work at which General Bonaparte set foot within Notre Dame the *Ambrosian Hymn of Praise* should burst forth from all sides, and that at its close the standards of the victorious army should be taken up to the altar, there to be blessed, amid the beating of drums, salvos of artillery, and the performance of martial music. We are thus, says Dr. Pohl, enabled to account for the employment of the triple choir, as well as for the peculiar direction, prefixed to the full score, that the orchestra and double choir should be placed at one end of the church and the organ at the other ; further, that the third choir (children) is to be stationed on a separate platform at some distance from the orchestra and double choir, because it represents the congregation, which from time to time takes part in the ecclesiastical ceremony. Finally, it explains the thoroughly original employment of military drums in the *Judex Crederis* and its being complimented by a march *Pour la présentation des Drapeaux.*

Berlioz in his Memoirs has several references to his work. In a letter to General Lwoff, dated February 23, 1849, he writes : "I am now hard at work upon a grand *Te Deum* for double chorus, with orchestra and organ *obbligato.* It is already assuming some sort of shape ; and I have work enough for two months yet, as there will be seven long movements." The work was not produced until 1855, and then not in honor of Napoleon, but by way of a preliminary, the day before, to the opening of the *Palais de l'Industrie.* For this reason the work now bears the dedication to the Prince Consort, of England, as the originator of such expositions. This was the only performance of the *Te Deum* during the composer's lifetime. On the 30th of April, 1855, it was given in the Church of St. Eustache, Paris, under his own direction. Writing to his son on April 25th, 1855, Berlioz says : "We heard the first orchestral rehearsal yesterday at St. Eustache, with the six hundred children. To-day I try the *ensemble* of my two hundred artist choristers. The thing goes well. It is colossal ... There is a *finale* grander than the *Tuba Mirum* of my *Requiem.*" With the result of its first performance he seems to have been thoroughly satisfied, for he wrote to his friend A. Morel : "The effect which the performance of the *Te Deum* produced, both upon myself and the executants, was enormous. Speaking generally, the measured grandeur of the conception and style made an immense impression upon them, and you may rest assured that the *Tibi Omnes* and the *Judex,* in two entirely different styles, are movements worthy of Babylon or Nineveh, and they will be still more imposing when they are heard in a smaller and less resonant space than that of the Church of St. Eustache."

The subsequent history of the work may be thus given in summary. A single movement, *Tibi omnes* (No. 2), was performed in the Palais de l'Industrie, and a partial performance of the work was given by Berlioz at Bordeaux. The *Judex Crederis* (No. 6) was performed under Berlioz' own direction at Baden Baden in August, 1857 ; but the work as an entirety was not heard again until November, 1863, when it was given in the Cathedral of Bordeaux. It was then given in Weimar and Vienna in the following year. Berlioz laid out his score on an extraordinary grand scale, viz., for three choirs, orchestra and organ. For its performance he required an orchestra of 134 executants, two choirs (each of 100 voices), a third choir of 600 children, and a grand organ. In a note prefixed to the full score he directed that the orchestra and two principal choirs, with the third choir on a separate platform and at some distance from them, were to be placed at one end of the church and the organ at the other. An analysis of the work is as follows :—

I.—TRIPLE CHORUS.

Te Deum laudamus: te Dominum confitemur.	We praise thee, O God: We acknowledge thee to be the Lord.
Te, æternum Patrem, omnis terra veneratur.	All the earth doth worship thee: the Father everlasting.

The First Movement, a Hymn of Praise (*Allegro moderato*, in F major, 4-4), opens with an instrumental Prelude, consisting of massive chords for the Orchestra, responded to by the Organ, and leading immediately to a triple chorus, treated for the most part in the manner of a double fugue. At the commencement two subjects are worked out contrapuntally. A second section, of a remarkable, tuneful and sonorous character, and treated in close "imitation," soon follows. Both sections are then repeated, but with important modifications; and the Movement is brought to an end *pianissimo* with a pause on F sharp, leading directly to the Second Movement (in B major).

II.—TRIPLE CHORUS.

Tibi omnes Angeli: tibi Cœli et Potestates;	To thee all Angels cry aloud: the Heavens and all the Powers herein;
Tibi Cherubim et Seraphim incessabili voce proclamant:	To thee Cherubim and Seraphim continually do cry,
Sanctus, Sanctus, Sanctus, Deus Sabaoth!	Holy, Holy, Holy: Lord God of Sabaoth;
Pleni sunt cœli et terra majestatis gloriæ tuæ.	Heaven and Earth are full of the majesty of thy glory.
Te gloriosus chorus Apostolorum.	The glorious company of the Apostles praise thee.
Te Prophetarum laudabilis numerus,	
Te Martyrum candidatus laudat exercitus.	The goodly fellowship of the Prophets praise thee.

Te per orbem terrarum sancta confitetur
Ecclesia,
Patrem immensæ majestatis;
Venerandum tuum verum et unicum Fi-
lium,
Sanctum quoque Paracletum Spiritum.

The noble army of Martyrs praise thee.
The holy Church throughout all the
world doth acknowledge thee;
The Father of an infinite Majesty;
Thine honorable, true, and only Son;
Also the Holy Ghost, the Comforter.

This is also a Hymn of Praise (*Andantino*, in B major, 3-4), and commences with an Organ Prelude. The first three verses are assigned to women's voices, the full choir entering at the words *Pleni sunt cæli et terra*. The next three verses, commencing *Te gloriosus chorus Apostolorum*, are appropriately sung by men's voices alone. Then the *Sanctus* is repeated by the Sopranos and Tenors of the two principal choirs, the entire triple choir joining in it on a repetition of *Pleni sunt cæli*. A third great section commences at the words *Te per orbem*, with a solo for the Basses; after which, with the re-entry of the full double chorus, the *Sanctus* is heard for the third time, but with entirely different treatment. A culminating point is reached by its being reinforced by the third choir; but the Movement ends quietly with a repetition of the opening Organ prelude, now transferred to the Orchestra.

III.--DOUBLE CHORUS.

Dignare, Domine, die isto, sine peccato
nos custodire.
Æterna fac cum Sanctis tuis in gloria
numerari.
Miserere nostri! miserere nostri!

Vouchsafe, O Lord, to keep us this day
without sin.
Make us to be numbered with thy Saints
in glory everlasting.
O Lord, have mercy upon us, have mercy
upon us.

The Third Movement (*Moderato*, in D major, 4-4) has all the characteristics of a fervent Prayer, and by its tranquility appropriately contrasts with what has gone before. It opens with a dialogue between Organ and Orchestra, the effect of which, when they answer each other from a distance, as Berlioz desired, must be very striking. The voices sing *sotto voce* almost throughout; the Organ is often prominent, but the Brass is very sparingly used.

IV.—DOUBLE CHORUS.

Tu Christe, Rex gloriæ;
Patris sempiternus Filius.

Tu, devicto mortis aculeo, aperuisti cre-
dentibus regna cœlorum.

Thou art the King of glory, O Christ.
Thou art the everlasting Son of the
Father.
When thou hadst overcome the sharp-
ness of death, thou didst open the
kingdom of Heaven to all believers.

Tu, ad liberandum suscepturus hominem, non horruisti Virginis uterum.	When thou tookest upon thee to deliver man, thou didst not abhor the Virgin's womb.
Tu ad dexteram Dei sedes, in gloria Patris.	Thou sittest at the right hand of God, in the glory of the Father.

The Fourth Movement (*Allegro non troppo*, in D major, ₵) is a Hymn of Praise. It commences with a vigorous theme for the Tenors and Basses, soon to be taken up by the Sopranos. Its middle section, commencing (in B minor) with the words *ad liberandum*, is in calm contrast to the rest. A new subject of a bright and animated character enters with *Tu ad dexteram*, and, after a reversion to the opening theme of the movement, is developed at length and maintained to the end. Throughout this chorus the Organ is silent.

V.—TENOR SOLO AND DOUBLE CHORUS.

Te ergo, qæsumus, famulis tuis subveni, quos pretioso sanguine redemisti.	We therefore pray thee, help thy servants, whom thou hast redeemed with thy precious blood.
Fiat misericordia tua, Domine, super nos, quemadmodum speravimus in te.	O Lord, let thy mercy lighten upon us, as our trust is in thee.

The Fifth Movement (*Andantino quasi Adagio*, in G minor and major, 3-4) is a heartfelt Prayer. An orchestral Prelude leads to the Solo, a long drawn out melody, accompanied by a continuous syncopated figure on the part of the Strings, and from time to time broken in upon by the upper Wood-wind and English Horn with melodious passages derived from and responding to it. After a full close in G minor, the Sopranos and Altos monotone the words *Fiat super nos*, etc., against a syncopated passage for Cornets and Trombones (*pianissimo*)—a device as remarkable for its originality as for its melodic and harmonic charm. The Solo is again taken up (now in B flat) and again twice responded to by the Sopranos and Altos with the passage last alluded to. With a modulation to G major, at the words *Speravimus in te*, the movement becomes more animated, and the Tenors of both choirs join in. Thus it is not till the Coda, in which the Basses take part, is reached that the full double chorus is heard. This Coda—a chorale-like passage, rich in old ecclesiastical harmonies—is sung throughout *pianissimo* and unaccompanied.

VI.—TRIPLE CHORUS.

Judex crederis esse venturus.	We believe that thou shalt come to be our Judge.
In te, Domine, speravi ! non confundar in æternum.	O Lord, in thee have I trusted ; let me never be confounded.
Salvum fac populum tuum et benedic hereditati tuæ, Domine.	O Lord, save thy people, and bless thine heritage.
Per singulos dies benedicimus, laudamus te, et laudamus nomen tuum.	Day by day we magnify thee, we worship thy Name, ever world without end.

In the Sixth and last Choral Movement (*Allegretto*, in B flat minor and major, 9–8) Praise and Prayer are combined. Its style, as Richard Pohl has remarked in the article already alluded to, is thoroughly characteristic of Berlioz; imposing by its general structure and strongly marked rhythm, surprising by the sharp contrasts it presents; and powerful by its vocal and instrumental combinations. The principal theme, the strongly marked rhythm of which runs throughout the greater part of the Movement, is given out by the Organ Solo. A counter-theme (in B flat minor) enters at the words *Salvum fac populum*. With singular persistency and boldness the first bar of this is subsequently taken up by the Orchestra (in D flat major) and made to serve as a continuous figure of accompaniment to the Prayer, *Per singulos dies*. With the return of the opening theme a powerful *crescendo* begins, and military Drums re-inforce the rhythm. Subsequently the Double-Drum takes up the same rhythm; the Cymbals join in with it at the words *Non confundar in æternum;* a wondrous climax is reached, and this massively conceived Movement is soon brought to a close with jubilant *fanfares* for Cornets and Trumpets.

VII.—MARCH.

Pour la Présentation des Drapeaux.

The March, by which the *Te Deum* is supplemented, though pompous and festive, is at the same time pervaded by a solemn and religious character. In its course the two principal themes of the opening movement of the *Te Deum* are introduced with striking effect, and thus serve in a singularly felicitous manner to establish its close connection with the *Te Deum* by which it has been preceded, and in a thoroughly artistic and satisfactory manner to round off, and impart a sense of uniformity to, the work as an organic whole.

ELIJAH.

MENDELSSOHN.

ORATORIO FOR SOLI, CHORUS AND ORCHESTRA.

OF three Oratorios which Mendelssohn wrote, namely, the *Hymn of Praise*, *St. Paul* and *Elijah*, the last named marks a distinct deviation from the more conventional form. So strongly does the dramatic element predominate throughout this work that Mendelssohn may be looked upon as the founder of a new and distinct oratorio school. In writing to Schubring on the subject of the book in 1838 he says :—" I am anxious to do justice to the dramatic element and, as yo say, no epic narrative must be introduced." And a little later he again writes :— " In such a character as that of *Elijah*, like every one in the Old Testament (except, perhaps, Moses), it appears to me that the dramatic should predominate; the personage should be introduced as acting and speaking with fervor, not, however, for heaven's sake, to become mere musical pictures, but inhabitants of a positive, practical world, such as we see in every chapter of the Old Testament." Mendelssohn has been so eminently successful in carrying out this design of making the dramatic element prominent that his work might, without difficulty, be staged and produced as a sacred opera, and with scenery, costumes and proper stage appointments would undoubtedly prove effective.

Mendelssohn conceived the idea of the Oratorio of *Elijah* in 1837, though the work was not completed until 1846, when on the 26th of August of that year it was first produced in Birmingham, England. Hiller tells us that the idea of the Oratorio was first suggested to Mendelssohn's mind by a verse in the nineteenth chapter of the First Book of Kings, "Behold, the Lord passed by," and that Mendelssohn after reading this verse said to him :—" Would not that be splendid for an Oratorio?" He discussed the subject with his friend Carl Klingemann in London in 1837, and the following year with Pastor Julius Schubring. It was during this year that his friend the Pastor assisted him in selecting some of the passages and in sketching out some of the scenes. During the next two years the work occupied Mendelssohn's mind, but it was not until 1840 that he really began to put it into a definite form. In 1842 he was still working at the book, and when in 1844 he received an invitation to conduct the Musical Festival at Birmingham in 1846 he decided to complete the work for that occasion, and bent his energies towards the fulfillment of that end (purpose).

The text is compiled from the First Book of Kings. It was written in German and afterwards translated into English by Mr. Bartholomew. The entire first part of the work and some half a dozen numbers of the second were completed and sent to Mr. Bartholomew by the 23d of May, 1846, and before the end of July the entire work was in the hands of the translator. On the 18th of August Mendelssohn arrived in London and made his home, as was his custom, with his friend Klingemann. He at once arranged for rehearsals of the work. The first (in England), with pianoforte accompaniment, took place at the house of Moscheles, and two others, with full band, followed at the Hanover Square Rooms. On the 23d of August, in company with Moscheles, he went to Birmingham. Moscheles was engaged to conduct the other works, which were Haydn's *Creation*, on the 25th, and Handel's *Messiah* and Beethoven's Mass in D on the 27th. Mendelssohn conducted two full rehearsals of his work on the 24th and 25th of August, and on the 26th the Oratorio was performed in public for the first time.

The Overture to *Elijah* is preceded by a short recitative as an Introduction, sung by Elijah, in which he proclaims the drought which is to last for three years. In the overture which immediately follows a musical description is given of the beginning of the drying up of the streams, and the consequent suffering of the people. It leads without interruption into the first chorus, in which the people in their distress call upon the Lord and in their trouble and need ask : " Wilt Thou quite destroy us ?" The distress of the people is further made known in the recitative : " The deeps afford no water ; the suckling's tongue now cleaveth for thirst to his mouth ; the infant children ask for bread, and there is no one breaketh it to them."

This is followed by (No. 2) a beautiful and touching supplication of the people, written as a solo duet for first and second soprano with chorus, " Lord, bow down Thine ear." Following this is the recitative for tenor, which is the admonition of Obadiah, " Ye people, rend your hearts and not your garments," after which comes the well known tenor air, " If with all your hearts," every note of which is full of consolation and comfort. The first part of the chorus following this beautiful tenor solo shows the prayers of the people still unanswered, and they cry in their exceeding need, " Yet doth the Lord see it not ; He mocketh at us." But in the latter part of the chorus a beautiful choral, beginning with the words : " For He is a jealous God," is most effectively introduced, showing the people still have hope and faith in the justice and mercy of Jehovah.

An angel now appears and commands Elijah to depart to the brook of Cherith. The angel sings the command in recitative, and with an alto voice, and this is followed by a melodious and beautifully written double quartet of angels, "For He shall give His angels charge over thee." The angel now commands Elijah (recitative) to arise and go to Zarephath, where he will be sustained by the widow woman, whose barrel of meal shall not waste nor cruse of oil fail until the day the Lord sendeth rain upon the earth. The first soprano solo is heard directly after this. In it the widow woman, in pathetic and appealing measures, supplicates the Prophet to succor and restore her son to her. Elijah's fervent intercession in behalf of the bereaved mother, the prayer answered and the passionate joy of the woman at the raising of her son follows.

The dramatic element, which Mendelssohn was so desirous should predominate in this work, is exemplified in this scene of the raising of the widow's son. After the chorus " Blessed are the men who fear Him " comes a recitative, in which Elijah declares, the three years being fulfilled, he will present himself before Ahab. In the scenes which follow, the dramatic, as well as the musical, element is worked up to a really splendid climax. Elijah appears before Ahab and the king accuses Elijah as being " he that troubleth Israel." Elijah answers, " I never troubled Israel's peace. It is thou, Ahab, and all thy father's house." Elijah asks that the whole of Israel assemble at Mount Carmel, and he challenges the Priests of Baal to offer sacrifice, the answer to be by fire from heaven. The challenge is accepted and the people take up the exciting double chorus, " Baal, we cry to thee." At the close Elijah commands them to "Call him louder," and with ever increasing energy they call yet again. Elijah taunts them further and again bids them to "Call him louder! He heareth not! Not a voice will answer you, none will listen, none heed you." Goaded on to fury, the Priests of Baal again renew their call to their god. They shout to him and pause in silence to listen for an answer. None comes. Again they shout and demand, " Hear and answer !" Again they pause and listen, but they receive no answer.

In strong contrast to these choruses of the wild and idolatrous worshippers of Baal comes the aria " Lord, God of Abraham," sung by Elijah. The pure and devotional character of this air and the lovely quartet " Cast thy burden upon the Lord," which follows it, is rendered more apparent and effective by way of contrast from what has just gone before and that which follows when the fire, at the command of Elijah, descends upon his sacrifice and the people burst into an exulting chorus, which is brought to a close by a fine choral and Elijah commands all the false prophets to be slain. The well known bass aria follows, " Is not His word like fire ?" sung by Elijah, and an arioso of rare beauty for alto, " Woe unto them." Obadiah now comes forward and reminds Elijah of the distress of the people, and asks him to help them. Elijah and later the people supplicate that the heavens may be opened and help afforded them. Three times a youth is sent up to look towards the sea and tell the famishing people if deliverance is nigh. The third time the little cloud, like a man's hand, is seen, which comes on and on, and in the orchestra is heard the rushing of the storm and the wind, and above this the joyous chorus of the people, singing " Thanks be to God." With this the first part is brought to a close.

PART II.—The second part of *Elijah* begins with the aria for soprano, " Hear ye, Israel." The first part of this number (adagio) is broad, flowing and melodious ; and in it is heard the voice of pleading and of warning. This is followed by a short recitative, which leads at once into the second subject (allegro), which begins with a joyous burst of exaltation, " I, I am He that comforteth." Following this brilliant aria comes the chorus " Be not afraid," which is one of the finest in the work, the full chorus being accompanied by both orchestra and organ, with splendid effect. The second part (or subject) of this chorus is in fugue form, and is stirring and full of animation. It leads again into the first and beautiful phrase, and closes with the choral "Thy help is near." In the next number, which is a recitative, Elijah speaks to Ahab and tells him of the evil he has done, and for this, and because he has caused Israel to sin, therefore the Lord will smite him, and the people under him, "And thou shalt know that He is the Lord."

Queen Jezebel now comes upon the scene, and endeavors to incite the people against Elijah. Ahab, she tells them, is King of Israel, and yet Elijah's power is greater than the king's. She accuses the Prophet of conspiring against Israel, and vows that she will have his life for those of her prophets he has sacrificed. She incites the people, who respond with vehemence that "He must perish." This duet and chorus leads into the chorus "Woe to him, he shall perish !" This entire scene is highly effective and of great dramatic power. Obadiah (tenor), in a beautiful recitative, tells Elijah of Jezebel's conspiracy against him, and warns him to flee for his life to the wilderness. The aria which follows, " It is enough," sung by the Man of God in his loneliness in the wilderness, is full of the most pathetic tenderness and sorrow. He prays that he may die, for though he has "been very zealous for the Lord" his work has been in vain and he begs: "Lord, take my life away." Overcome by grief and weariness, he sinks to sleep beneath a juniper tree, and the voices of three angels are heard in the lovely, unaccompanied trio "Lift thine eyes." This is followed by the chorus, of wondrous and suave beauty, " He watching over Israel," which is probably the most widely known chorus of the entire work. In a recitative for alto the Angel arouses Elijah and bids him go to Horeb. The Prophet, on hearing the command, again bewails that his labor has been in vain, and pleads for death. The answer comes in one of the most beautiful vocal compositions ever penned by Mendelssohn, " Oh, rest in the Lord."

The music to this number is of the most elevated character, and worthy of the words which inspired it. Every phrase speaks comfort and consolation, and the noble chorus " He that shall endure to the end " is worthy to follow it. The next recitative is declaimed by Elijah, and in it he calls upon the Lord : " My soul is thirsting for Thee," for he has regained his courage and his zeal. The Angel bids him arise and stand on the mount before the Lord, " For there His glory will appear and shine on thee ! Thy face must be veiled, for He draweth near." The chorus which follows is intensely realistic, and, while dramatic, is full of devotional spirit and most impressive. The Prophet must be pictured veiled, waiting the coming of Jehovah. The soprano and alto chorus, with mighty voice, proclaim :

"Behold! God the Lord passed by!" As if awed by holy fear, the chorus begin, in the softest strains, increasing in power, "And a mighty wind rent the mountains around," and, decreasing again to pianissimo, tell us, without accompaniment of either orchestra or organ, "But yet the Lord was not in the tempest."

The earthquake and the fire pass by. The treatment of each subject is descriptive, and similar to the first. The chorus proclaim : "But yet the Lord was not in the fire." With a beautiful and effective musical modulation, and in the tenderest pianissimo, the chorus sings : "And after the fire there came a still, small voice, and in that still voice onward came the Lord." Following this comes a double quartet and chorus of the celestial choir, who sing : "Holy, holy, holy is God the Lord." Elijah is commanded to return upon his way, as the Lord has left seven thousand in Israel who have not bowed the knee to Baal. With readiness and zeal Elijah answers : "I go on my way in the strength of the Lord." This recitative precedes the aria sung by Elijah, "For the Mountains shall depart and the hills be removed," which prepares for the final chorus, in which the dramatic climax of the work is reached, in the description by the people of the coming of the fiery chariot and the whirlwind by which he is taken up to heaven. Following this effective chorus is an aria for tenor, "Then shall the righteous shine forth as the sun," and a recitative for soprano, which leads at once into the chorus "But the Lord from the North has raised one, who from the rising on his name shall call." The beautiful and melodious quartet "O come every one that thirsteth" is the next number, and the chorus "And then shall your Light break forth as the Light of the morning" is the final chorus of the work.

ELIJAH.

The author of this English Version has endeavored to render it as nearly in accordance with the Scriptural texts as the music to which it is adapted will admit. The references are, therefore, to be considered rather as authorities than quotations.

PART I.

INTRODUCTION.

Recitative.

ELIJAH.—As God the Lord of Israel liveth, before whom I stand, there shall not be dew nor rain these years, but according to my word.

1 Kings xvii. 1.

OVERTURE.

Chorus.

THE PEOPLE.—Help, Lord! wilt Thou quite destroy us?

The harvest now is over, the summer days are gone, and yet no power cometh to help us! Will then the Lord be no more God in Zion ?

Jeremiah viii. 20.

Recitative Chorus.

The deeps afford no water; and the rivers are exhausted! The suckling's tongue now cleaveth for thirst to his mouth: the infant children ask for bread, and there is no one breaketh it to feed them!

Lament. iv. 4.

Duet and Chorus.

THE PEOPLE.—Lord! bow thine ear to our prayer!

DUET.—Zion spreadeth her hands for aid; and there is neither help nor comfort.

Lament. i. 17.

Recitative.

OBADIAH.—Ye people, rend your hearts, and not your garments, for your transgressions the Prophet Elijah hath sealed the heavens through the word of God. I therefore say to ye, Forsake' your idols, return to God; for He is slow to anger, and merciful, and kind and gracious, and repenteth Him of the evil.

Joel ii. 12, 13.

Air.

If with all your hearts ye truly seek me, ye shall ever surely find me. Thus saith our God.

Oh! that I knew where I might find Him, that I might even come before His presence.

Deut. iv. 29.   Job xxiii. 3.

Chorus.

THE PEOPLE.—Yet doth the Lord see it not: He mocketh at us; His curse hath fallen down upon us; His wrath will pursue us, till He destroy us!

For He, the Lord our God, He is a jealous God; and He visiteth all the father's sins on the children to the third and fourth generation of them that hate Him. His mercies on thousands fall— fall on all them that love Him, and keep His commandments.

Deut. xxviii. 22.   Exodus xx. 5, 6.

Recitative.

AN ANGEL.—Elijah! get thee hence; depart, and turn thee eastward: thither hide thee by Cherith's brook. There shalt thou drink its waters; and the Lord thy God hath commanded the ravens to feed thee there: so do according unto His word.

1 Kings xvii. 3.

Double Quartet.

ANGELS.—For He shall give His angels charge over thee; that they shall protect thee in all the ways thou goest; that their hands shall uphold and guide thee, lest thou dash thy foot against a stone.

Psalm xci. 11, 12.

Recitative.

AN ANGEL.—Now Cherith's brook is dried up, Elijah arise and depart, and get thee to Zarephath; thither abide: for the Lord hath commanded a widow woman there to sustain thee. And the barrel of meal shall not waste, neither shall the cruse of oil fail, until the day that the Lord sendeth rain upon the earth.

1 Kings xvii. 7, 9, 14.

Recitative and Air.

THE WIDOW.—What have I to do with thee, O man of God? art thou come to me, to call my sin unto remembrance? —to slay my son art thou come hither? Help me, man of God! my son is sick! and his sickness is so sore, that there is no breath left in him! I go mourning all the day long; I lie down and weep at night. See mine affliction. Be thou the orphan's helper!

ELIJAH.—Give me thy son. Turn unto her, O Lord my God; in mercy help this widow's son! For Thou art gracious, and full of compassion, and plenteous in mercy and truth. Lord, my God, O let the spirit of this child return, that he again may live!

THE WIDOW.—Wilt thou show wonders to the dead? Shall the dead arise and praise thee?

ELIJAH.—Lord, my God, O let the spirit of this child return, that he again may live!

THE WIDOW.—The Lord hath heard thy prayer, the soul of my son reviveth!

ELIJAH.—Now behold, thy son liveth!

THE WIDOW.—Now by this I know that thou art a man of God, and that His word in thy mouth is the truth. What shall I render to the Lord for all His benefits to me?

BOTH.—Thou shalt love the Lord thy God with all thine heart, and with all thy soul, and with all thy might. O blessed are they who fear Him!

1 Kings xvii. 17, 18, 21—24. Job x. 15. Psalm xxxviii. 6; vi. 7; x. 14; lxxxvi. 15, 16; lxxxviii. 10; cxxviii. 1.

Chorus.

Blessed are the men who fear Him: they ever walk in the ways of peace. Through darkness riseth light to the upright. He is gracious, compassionate; He is righteous.

Psalm cxxviii. 1; cxii. 1, 4.

Recitative.

ELIJAH.—As God the Lord of Sabaoth liveth, before whom I stand, three years this day fulfilled, I will show myself unto Ahab; and the Lord will then send rain again upon the earth.

AHAB.—Art thou Elijah? art thou he that troubleth Israel?

CHORUS.—Thou art Elijah, he that troubleth Israel!

ELIJAH.—I never troubled Israel's peace: it is thou, Ahab, and all thy father's house. Ye have forsaken God's commands; and thou hast followed Baalim!

Now send and gather to me, the whole of Israel unto Mount Carmel: there summon the prophets of Baal, and also the prophets of the groves, who are feasted at Jezebel's table. Then we shall see whose God is the Lord.

CHORUS.—And then we shall see whose God is God the Lord.

ELIJAH.—Rise then, ye priests of Baal : select and slay a bullock, and put no fire under it : uplift your voices, and call the god ye worship ; and I then will call on the Lord Jehovah : and the God who by fire shall answer, let him be God.

CHORUS.—Yea ; and the God who by fire shall answer, let him be God.

ELIJAH.—Call first upon your god : your numbers are many : I, even I, only remain, one prophet of the Lord ! Invoke your forest-gods and mountain-deities.

1 Kings xvii. 17 ; xviii. 1, 15, 18, 19, 23—25.

Chorus.

PRIESTS OF BAAL.—Baal, we cry to thee ! hear and answer us ! Heed the sacrifice we offer ! hear us ! O hear us, Baal!

Hear, mighty god ! Baal, O answer us ! Let thy flames fall and extirpate the foe ! O hear us, Baal !

Recitative.

ELIJAH.—Call him louder, for he is a god ! He talketh ; or he is pursuing ; or he is in a journey ; or, peradventure, he sleepeth ; so awaken him : call him louder.

Chorus.

PRIESTS OF BAAL.—Hear our cry, O Baal ! now arise ! wherefore slumber ?

Recitative and Air.

ELIJAH.—Call him louder ! he heareth not. With knives and lancets cut yourselves after your manner : leap upon the altar ye have made : call him, and prophecy ! Not a voice will answer you ; none will listen, none heed you.

Chorus.

PRIESTS OF BAAL.—Hear and answer, Baal ! Mark ! how the scorner derideth us ! Hear and answer !

1 Kings xviii. 1, 15, 17, 18, 19, 23—29.

Recitative and Air.

ELIJAH.—Draw near, all ye people: come to me !

Lord God of Abraham, Isaac, and Israel ! this day let it be known that Thou art God; and I am Thy servant ! O show to all this people that I have done these things according to Thy word ! O hear me, Lord, and answer me; and show this people that Thou art Lord God; and let their hearts again be turned !

1 Kings xviii. 30, 36, 37.

Quartet.

ANGELS.—Cast thy burden upon the Lord, and He shall sustain thee. He never will suffer the righteous to fall: He is at thy right hand.

Thy mercy, Lord, is great; and far above the heavens. Let none be made ashamed that wait upon Thee !

Psalm lv. 22; xvi. 8; cviii. 5; xxv. 3.

Recitative.

ELIJAH.—O Thou, who makest Thine angels spirits;—Thou, whose ministers are flaming fires, let them now descend !

Psalm civ. 4.

Chorus.

THE PEOPLE.—The fire descends from heaven; the flames consume his offering !

Before Him upon your faces fall ! The Lord is God : O Israel hear ! Our God is one Lord: and we will have no other gods before the Lord !

1 Kings xviii. 38, 39.

Recitative.

ELIJAH.—Take all the prophets of Baal; and let not one of them escape you: bring them down to Kishon's brook, and there let them be slain.

Chorus.

THE PEOPLE.—Take all the prophets of Baal; and let not one of them escape us: bring all, and slay them !

1 Kings xviii. 40.

Air.

ELIJAH.—Is not His word like a fire: and like a hammer that breaketh the rock into pieces ?

For God is angry with the wicked every day: and if the wicked turn not, the Lord will whet His sword; and He hath bent His bow, and made it ready.

Jer. xxiii. 29.   Psalm vii. 11, 12.

Air.

Woe unto them who forsake Him ! destruction shall fall upon them, for they have transgressed against Him. Though they are by Him redeemed, yet they have spoken falsely against him.

Hosea vii. 13.

Recitative and Chorus.

OBADIAH.—O man of God, help thy people ! Among the Idols of the Gentiles, are they any that can command the rain, or cause the heavens to give their showers ? The Lord our God alone can do these things.

ELIJAH.—O Lord, thou hast overthrown thine enemies and destroyed them. Look down on us from heaven, O Lord; regard the distress of Thy people: open the heavens and send us relief: help, help Thy servant now, O God !

THE PEOPLE.—Open the heavens and send us relief: help, help Thy servant now, O God !

ELIJAH.—Go up now, child, and look toward the sea. Hath my prayer been heard by the Lord?

THE YOUTH.—There is nothing. The heavens are as brass above me.

ELIJAH.—When the heavens are closed up because they have sinned against Thee, yet if they pray and confess Thy name, and turn from their sin when Thou dost afflict them; then hear from heaven, and forgive the sin; Help! send Thy servant help, O God!

THE PEOPLE.—Then hear from heaven, and forgive the sin! Help! send Thy servant help, O Lord!

ELIJAH.—Go up again, and still look toward the sea.

THE YOUTH.—There is nothing. The earth is as iron under me!

ELIJAH.—Hearest thou no sound of rain?—seest thou nothing arise from the deep?

THE YOUTH.—No; there is nothing.

ELIJAH.—Have respect to the prayer of Thy servant, O Lord, my God! Unto Thee will I cry, Lord, my rock; be not silent to me; and Thy great mercies remember, Lord!

THE YOUTH.—Behold, a little cloud ariseth now from the waters; it is like a man's hand! The heavens are black with clouds and with wind: the storm rusheth louder and louder!

THE PEOPLE.—Thanks be to God, for all His mercies!

ELIJAH.—Thanks be to God, for He is gracious, and His mercy endureth for evermore!

> Jer. xiv. 22. 2 Chron. vi. 19, 26, 27.
> Deut. xxviii. 23. Psalm xxviii. 1; cvi. 1.
> 1 Kings xviii. 43, 45.

Chorus.

Thanks be to God! He laveth the thirsty land! The waters gather; they rush along; they are lifting their voices!
The stormy billows are high; their fury is mighty. But the Lord is above them, and almighty!

> Psalm xciii. 3, 4.

PART II.

Air.

Hear ye, Israel; hear what the Lord speaketh:—" Oh, hadst thou heeded my commandments!"
Who hath believed our report; to whom is the arm of the Lord revealed?
Thus saith the Lord, the Redeemer of Israel, and his Holy One, to him oppressed by Tyrants: thus saith the Lord:—I am He that comforteth; be not afraid, for I am thy God, I will strengthen thee. Say, who art thou, that thou art afraid of a man that shall die; and forgettest the Lord thy Maker, who had stretched forth the heavens, and laid the earth's foundations? Be not afraid, for I, thy God, will strengthen thee.

> Isaiah xlviii. 1, 18; liii. 1; xlix. 7; xli. 10;
> li. 12, 13.

Chorus.

Be not afraid, saith God the Lord. Be not afraid! thy help is near. God, the Lord thy God, saith unto thee, " Be not afraid!"
Though thousands languish and fall beside thee, and tens of thousands around thee perish, yet still it shall not come nigh thee.

> Isaiah xli. 10. Psalm xci. 7.

Recitative and Chorus.

ELIJAH.—The Lord hath exalted thee from among the people; and over his people Israel hath made thee king. But thou, Ahab, hast done evil to provoke him to anger above all that were before thee : as if it had been a light thing for thee to walk in the sins of Jeroboam. Thou hast made a grove and an altar to Baal, and served him and worshipped him. Thou hast killed the righteous, and also taken possession.

And the Lord shall smite all Israel, as a reed is shaken in the water; and He shall give Israel up and thou shalt know He is the Lord.

     1 Kings xiv. 7, 9, 15; xvi. 30, 31, 32, 33.

THE QUEEN.—Have you not heard he hath prophesied against all Israel?

CHORUS.—We heard it with our ears.

THE QUEEN.—Hath he not prophesied also against the King of Israel?

CHORUS.—We heard it with our ears.

THE QUEEN.—And why hath he spoken in the name of the Lord? Doth Ahab govern the kingdom of Israel while Elijah's power is greater than the king's?

The gods do so to me, and more ; if, by to-morrow about this time, I make not his life as the life of one of them whom he had sacrificed at the brook of Kishon !

CHORUS.—He shall perish !

THE QUEEN.—Hath he not destroyed Baal's prophets?

CHORUS.—He shall perish!

THE QUEEN.—Yea, by the sword he destroyed them all !

CHORUS —He destroyed them all !

THE QUEEN.—He also closed the heavens !

CHORUS.—He also closed the heavens!

THE QUEEN.—And called down a famine upon the land.

CHORUS.—And called down a famine upon the land.

THE QUEEN.—So go ye forth and seize Elijah, for he is worthy to die; slaughter him ! do unto him as he hath done !

Chorus.

Woe to him, he shall perish; for he closed the heavens! And why hath he spoken in the name of the Lord? Let the guilty prophet perish ! He hath spoken falsely against our land and us, as we have heard with our ears. So go ye forth ; seize on him ! He shall die !

     Jeremiah xxvi. 9, 11. 1 Kings xviii. 10; xix. 2; xxi. 7. Ecclesiastes xlviii. 2, 3.

Recitative.

OBADIAH.—Man of God, now let my words be precious in thy sight. Thus saith Jezebel: "Elijah is worthy to die." So the mighty gather against thee, and they have prepared a net for thy steps; that they may seize thee, that they may slay thee. Arise, then, and hasten for thy life; to the wilderness journey. The Lord thy God doth go with thee : He He will not fail thee, He will not forsake thee. Now begone, and bless me also.

ELIJAH.—Though stricken, they have not grieved! Tarry here, my servant: the Lord be with thee. I journey hence to the wilderness.

     2 Kings i. 13. Jer. v. 3; xxvi. 11. Psalm lix. 3. 1 Kings xix. 4. Deut. xxxi. 6. Exodous xii. 32. 1 Samuel xvii. 37.

Air.

ELIJAH.—It is enough, O Lord; now take away my life, for I am not better than my fathers ! I desire to live no longer: now let me die. for my days are but vanity !

I have been very jealous for the Lord God of Hosts! for the Children of Israel have broken Thy covenant, thrown down Thine altars, and slain Thy prophets with the sword: and I, even I, only am left; and they seek my life to take it away.

Job vii. 16. 1 Kings xix. 10.

Recitative.

See, now he sleepeth beneath a juniper tree in the wilderness: and there the angels of the Lord encamp round about all them that fear Him.

1 Kings xix. 5. Psalm xxxiv. 7.

Trio.

ANGELS.—Lift thine eyes to the mountains, whence cometh help. Thy help cometh from the Lord, the Maker of heaven and earth. He hath said, thy foot shall not be moved: thy Keeper will never slumber.

Psalm cxxi. 1, 3.

Chorus.

ANGELS.—He, watching over Israel, slumbers not, nor sleeps. Shouldst thou, walking in grief, languish, He will quicken thee.

Psalm cxxi. 4; cxxxviii. 7.

Recitative.

AN ANGEL.—Arise, Elijah, for thou hast a long journey before thee. Forty days and forty nights shalt thou go; to Horeb, the mount of God.

ELIJAH.—O Lord, I have labored in vain; yea, I have spent my strength for naught!
O that Thou wouldst rend the heavens, that Thou wouldst come down; that the mountains would flow down at Thy presence, to make Thy name known to Thine adversaries, through the wonders of Thy works!
O Lord, why hast Thou made them to err from Thy ways, and hardened their

hearts that they do not fear Thee? O that I now might die!

1 Kings xix. S. Isaiah xlix. 4; lxiv. 1, 2; lxiii. 7.

Air.

O rest in the Lord; wait patiently for Him, and He shall give thee thy heart's desires. Commit thy way unto Him, and trust in Him, and fret not thyself because of evil doers.

Psalm xxxvii. 1, 7.

Chorus.

He that shall endure to the end shall be saved.

Matthew xxiv. 13.

Recitative.

ELIJAH.—Night falleth round me, O Lord! Be Thou not far from me! hide not Thy face, O Lord, from me; my soul is thirsting for Thee, as a thirsty lane.

AN ANGEL.—Arise, now! get thee without, stand on the mount before the Lord; for there His glory will appear and shine on thee! Thy face must be veiled, for He draweth near.

Psalm cxliii. 6, 7. 1 Kings xix. 11.

Chorus.

Behold! God the Lord passed by! And a mighty wind rent the mountains around, break in pieces the rocks, break them before the Lord; but yet the Lord was not in the tempest.
Behold! God the Lord passed by! And the sea was upheaved, and the earth was shaken: but yet the Lord was not in the earthquake.
And after the earthquake there came a fire; but yet the Lord was not in the fire.
And after the fire there came a still, small voice; and in that still voice, onward came the Lord.

1 Kings xix. 11, 12.

Recitative.

Above Him stood the Seraphim, and one cried to another:

22   *Second Concert, Wednesday Evening.*

Quartet and Chorus.

ANGELS.—Holy, holy, holy is God the Lord—the Lord Sabaoth! Now His glory hath filled all the earth.

Isaiah vi. 2, 3.

Recitative.

CHORUS.—Go, return upon thy way! For the Lord yet hath left Him seven thousand in Israel, knees which have not bowed to Baal: go, return upon thy way; Thus the Lord commandeth.

ELIJAH.—I go on my way in the strength of the Lord. For Thou art my Lord; and I will suffer for Thy sake. My heart is therefore glad, my glory rejoiceth, and my flesh shall also rest in hope.

i Kings xix. 15, 18. Psalm lxxi. 16; xvi. 2, 9.

Air.

ELIJAH.—For the mountains shall depart, and the hills be removed; but Thy kindness shall not depart from me, neither shall the covenant of Thy peace be removed.

Isaiah liv. 10.

Chorus.

Then did Elijah the prophet break forth like a fire; his words appeared like burning torches. Mighty kings by him were overthrown. He stood on the mount of Sinai, and heard the judgments of the future; and in Horeb, its vengeance.

And when the Lord would take him away to heaven, lo! there came a fiery chariot, with fiery horses; and he went by whirlwind to heaven.

Ecclesiastes xlviii. 1, 6, 7. 2 Kings ii. 1, 11.

Air.

Then shall the righteous shine forth as the sun in their heavenly Father's realm. Joy on their head shall be for everlasting, and all sorrow and mourning shall flee away forever.

Matthew xiii. 43. Isaiah li. 11.

Recitative.

Behold, God hath sent Elijah the prophet, before the coming of the great and dreadful day of the Lord. And he shall turn the heart of the fathers to the children, and the heart of the children unto their fathers; lest the Lord shall come and smite the earth with a curse.

Malachi iv. 5, 6.

Chorus.

But the Lord, from the north hath raised one who from the rising of the sun shall call upon His name and come on princes.

Behold, my servant and mine elect, in whom my soul delighteth! On him the Spirit of God shall rest: the spirit of wisdom and understanding, the spirit of might and of counsel, the spirit of knowledge and of the fear of the Lord.

Isaiah xli. 25; xlii. 1; xi. 2.

Quartet.

O! come every one that thirsteth, O come to the waters: come unto Him. O hear, and your souls shall live for ever!

Isaiah lv. 1, 3.

Chorus.

And then shall your light break forth as the light of morning breaketh; and your health shall speedily spring forth then; and the glory of the Lord ever shall reward you.

Lord, our Creator, how excellent Thy name is in all the nations! Thy fillest heaven with Thy glory. Amen!

Isaiah lviii. 8. Psalm viii. 1.

The Marriage of Figaro.

MOZART.

OVERTURE; AND GRAND FINALE ACT II.

THE book of Mozart's opera *Le Nozze di Figaro* is taken from Beaumarchais's comedy *Le Mariage de Figaro, ou la folle Journee*, and is a continuation of the same author's comedy *Le Barbier de Seville*. In *Le Mariage de Figaro* we meet with the same personages with whom we have become familiar in *Le Barbier*, and make the acquaintance of several others. The Count Almaviva has married Rosina, the niece of Dr. Bartolo, and with him into his new establishment he has taken Figaro and Marcellina, the duenna of the once lively Rosina. Dr. Bartolo and Basillio are also met again—all with new surroundings. The new characters introduced are Susanna, the maid and confidant of the Countess Almaviva ; Cherubino, a page to the Count ; Antonio, a gardener, and his daughter, called in the comedy Fanchette, but in the libretto the name has been changed to Barbarina. The story which leads up to the *finale* of the second act is as follows :—

Figaro is betrothed to Susanna and preparations are in progress for the nuptials, when Figaro discovers that Susanna is the object of the Count's attentions. The Count has developed into a sad flirt as well as a most jealous husband since his marriage. Don Basillio is the tool of the Count in trying to forward the latter's attentions to Susanna. His Lordship has also shown a tender feeling for Barbarina, the gardener's daughter, and upon one occasion, when visiting her at her cottage, finds with her Cherubino, the Page, and as a punishment for poaching on his Lordship's preserves, dismisses the boy from his service. This Page Figaro determines to use as his assistant in a counterplot against the Count and Basillio, though Cherubino is unconscious that he is being made use of. After being dismissed by the Count, Cherubino seeks out Susanna to ask her to intercede with the Countess, who is his godmother and for whom he entertains a most ardent boyish passion, in his behalf. During this interview the Count enters, to press his suit with Susanna, and Cherubino quickly conceals himself behind a large armchair.

The Count is proceeding to make love to Susanna when footsteps are heard, and, not wishing to be found alone with her, he conceals himself behind the armchair, and as he does so Cherubino slips around into the chair and Susanna covers him with a gown belonging to the Countess, just as Basilio enters. The latter tries to advance his Lordship's suit, and in doing so mentions Cherubino and his passion for the Countess. This enrages the Count, who at once rises and demands to know the whole of the story which the gossiping Basilio has been insinuating, and threatens vengeance upon the Page. Susanna intercedes for him, whereupon the Count relates how he, only the morning before, had found the young scapegrace at the cottage of Barbarina, having suspected his presence there by finding the door of the cottage locked, and upon demanding entrance was further convinced by the tell-tale look on Barbarina's face. Seeking in every corner for him, his Lordship had finally lifted up the table cover. "Lo! the Page," he exclaims, and imitating the action described, he raises the gown on the armchair and discovers Cherubino.

The Count is about to inflict further punishment upon him when he remembers that the Page has heard him make love to Susanna. This fact secures pardon for the boy, and as there is a vacancy in his Lordship's regiment, Cherubino is given a commission and ordered to join it at once. Susanna informs the Countess of the Count's visit to her, and of all that Cherubino has overheard, and they assist Figaro in his plot to entrap the Count. Cherubino, having written a sonnet to 'the Countess, comes to take leave of her and sings his song, after which he is, in furtherance of Figaro's plans, to be arrayed in female dress. Susanna has completed the headdress and by the Countess's order has gone to fetch one of her gowns for the Page, when the Count's voice is heard; Cherubino runs and conceals himself in the closet. The Countess locks him in and then opens the door to the Count, whose jealousy is at once aroused by the confused manner of the Countess. He demands entrance to the closet where Cherubino is concealed. Leaving the room for a little time, Cherubino escapes by leaping from the window, and Susanna enters the closet. The Count returns with a crowbar to effect his entrance by force, and with it goes to the closet, and at this point the *finale* begins.

GRAND FINALE ACT II.

Count.
Come forth, you precious varlet!
Rogue, no longer hesitate!

Countess.
Oh, my lord, your growing anger
Makes me tremble for his fate.

Count.
Dare you still my wishes flout?

Countess.
No, but hear me.

Count.
Well, speak out!

Countess.
True, you'll p'r'aps have some suspicion,
When you find him—his condition—
Naked neck, and bare of bosom—

Count.

Nacked neck and bare of bosom !
And what further—

Countess.

He just put on woman's dress.

Count.

Oh I see it, worthless woman !
But I'll be avenged no less.

(Seizes the crowbar in a rage.)

Countess.

You insult me by your passion—
Wrong me by untrustfulness !

Count.

Give the key here.

Countess.

Spare your anger.
Know, he's guiltless –

Count.

I know nothing
Out of sight and knowledge human !
Faithless and abandoned woman ;
Go, no more dishonor me.

Countess.

I will go—but—

Count.

I despise you.

Countess.

I am pure.

Count.

Your face belies you.

(She gives him the key.)

I will kill him ; that no longer
He may plot such infamy.

Countess.

Ah, how far leads such blind passion !
Where will end the agony ?

(The Count opens the door ; the Countess flings
herself into a chair, covering her eyes. Susanna
comes out of the closet with ironical gravity.)

Count and *Countess.*

Susanna !

Susanna.

My master !
Is any disaster ?

But take up your sword, then,
And slay him, my lord, then,
The Page whom you doubt.

Countess.

What means this contrivance ?

(Susanna comes out.)

Count. .

(Some cunning connivance !
My head whirls about.)

Susanna.

(Then both the contrivance
Has bothered, no doubt.)

Count.

Alone, too ?

Susanna.

Examine—He's probably here.

Count.

I'll seek him, I'll seek him,
And find him, no fear.

(Enters the closet. The Countess rises.)

Countess.

Susanna, I'm quaking ;
My strength is forsaking—

Susanna.

Take courage, show spirit,
He's off safe and clear.

(The Count returns confused.)

Count.

How strange is my error ;
I scarce can believe it ;
But if I caused terror
I beg you'll forgive it.

(To the Countess.)

Such joking is cruel,
Too cruel I call it.

Countess.

Your folly deserves, sir—

Susanna.

No pity at all.

Count.

I love you.

Countess.

Oh, fie, sir !

Count.
I swear it!

Countess.
Mere words, sir :
I'm false : in your fever
You called me deceiver.

Count.
Susanna, pray help me
My peace to repair.

Susanna.
A man of suspicion
Well merits such fare.

Countess.
And all this commotion
Rewards the devotion
Of one who so loves you
And hoped love to share!

Susanna.
My lady!

Count.
Rosina!

Countess.
O silence!
Most cruel of husbands,
To utter that name:
You wound—you despise me—
You put me to shame!
A wife your suspicion
Will drive to despair!

Susanna.
(Aside to the Countess.)
You see his repentance,
Commute now his sentence;
Forgive and forget.

Countess.
I can't bring my conscience
To pardon him yet.

Count.
But the Page you confessed to?

Countess.
'Twas only to test you.

Count.
Your fright—your confusion—

Countess.
Why, that was a jest, too.

Count.
But this villainous billet? (Showing it.)

Countess.
'Tis Figaro's letter,
And sent through Basillio—

Count.
The rogues! I'm their debtor.

Countess.
He earns not forgiveness
Who grace can't bestow.

Count.
Well, well, if 'twill suit you,
Peace shall be mutual,
You won't be inflexible,
Dearest, I know.

Countess.
Susanna, I render
A heart much too tender.
The wrath of a woman,
Who credits now this ?

Susanna.
The men, ma'am, discern 'em :
We twist and we turn 'em ;
At most the transaction
Winds up with a kiss.

Count.
Regard me!

Countess.
Unkind one !

Count.
Yes, I was the blind one—
The deed I abjure.

Count. Countess. Susanna.

I ⎫
You ⎬ Ever will hold ⎰ You.
He ⎭ ⎱ Me.
  Her.
All stainless and pure.
(Enter Figaro.)

Figaro.
My lord, the musicians;
All sort and conditions

Of music; fifes squealing
And trumpet's loud pealing;
Your vassals advancing,
With singing and dancing,
To honor the wedding,
To which we'll repair.
(The Count stops him as he is going.)

Count.
Come here, and less prating.

Figaro.
The people are waiting.

Count.
Ere going resolve me
A doubt which I share.

Countess. Susanna. Figaro.
(Aside.)
Now here comes a poser;
And what shall we say?

Count.
(Aside.)
The cards in my hand I
Must skillfully play.
Can you tell me who indited
This same note, Sir Figaro?

Figaro.
No, I can't, sir.

Countess. Susanna.
What, you can't, sir!

Figaro.
No, I can't tell; no, no, no!

Susanna.
Why, you gave it Don Basilio.

Countess.
To deliver, you remember.

Figaro.
Oh I swear it wasn't so.

Susanna.
How? You know of that young spark in
Yonder garden, and the larking—

Count.
You assert then—

Figaro.
I dont know.

Count.
Oh, you cannot disabuse us,
For your face your guilt accuses.
And I see you want to lie.

Figaro.
It's my face, not me, that's lying.

Countess. Susanna.
Vainly you your wits are trying,
We the secret have discovered
And you need not make reply.

Count.
Now, what say you ?

Figaro.
Deuce a bit, sir.

Count.
You admit, then ?

Figaro.
Don't admit, sir.

Countess. Susanna.
There, confess, mad-witted joker ;
It is time the farce had ceased.

Figaro.
Well, to make an end dramatic,
Theater usage says emphatic,
You should wind up all the business
With a matrimonial feast.

Countess. Susanna.
Good, my lord, do not oppose it,
To our wishes yield, we pray.

Count.
(Aside.)
Marcellina, Marcellina !
What can make her longer stay ?
(Enter Antonio intoxicated, bringing in a pot of
flowers with the stalks broken.)

Antonio.
Oh, my lord, my lord !

Count.
What's happened ?

Antonio.
'Twas a knave's trick. But who did it ?

All Four.

What's the grievance?   What's the matter?

Antonio.

Listen to me.

All.

Well, continue.

Antonio.
(To the Count.)

From the lattice o'er the garden
Often they pitch out their rubbish,
And not long ago the beggars
Pitched a man out of the window.

Count. Countess. Susanna.

From the lattice!

Antonio.

See the flowers!

Count.

In the garden!

Countess. Susanna.
(Aside.)

Help us, Figaro.

Count.

What means this?

Countess. Susanna.
(Aside.)

The knave confounds us.

Countess. Susanna. Figaro.

But what would this drunkard with us?

Count.
(To Antonio.)

So, a man? And 'vhither went he?

Antonio.

Helter skelter fleet the rascal,
And I lost him in a moment.

Susanna.
(Aside to Figaro.)

'Twas the Page, you know.

Figaro.
(Aside.)

I know it. Ha, ha, ha!

Count.

Come, silence, silence!

Antonio.

Why do you laugh?

Figaro.

Ho, ho, ho!

Count.

Silence!

Figaro.
(To Antonio.)

You've been drunk since break of morning.

Count.
(To Antonio.)

Just repeat the tale.—A man fell
From the window?

Antonio.

From the window.

Count.

To the garden?

Antonio.

To the garden.

Countess. Susanna. Figaro.

'Tis the wine, my lord, speaks in him.

Count.

Well, you recognize his features?

Antonio.

Not I.

Countess. Susanna.
(Aside.)

Figaro, be careful.

Figaro.
(To Antonio.)

Stop your whisperings, you rascal,
Making all this noise and nonsense.
(Pointing to the flowers.)
There's no use of further hiding :
It was I who jumped down yonder.

Count. Antonio.

You? What, you!

Countess. Susanna.

What brains! What quickness!

Figaro.

Why do you stare?

Count.
(Aside.)

I don't believe him.

Antonio.

What has made you grow so big since?
You were not so big in jumping.

Figaro.

Pooh! that happens oft to jumpers.

Antonio.

Who'd ha' thought it!

Countess. Susanna.
(To Antonio.)

Ass, don't argue.

Count.
(To Antonio.)

What say you?

Antonio.

Oh, well, I fancied
I was the youngster—

Count.

Cherubino!

Countess. Susanna.
(Aside.)

Plague upon him!

Figaro.

Very likely;
He's on horseback come from Seville:
Just arrived: it's him most surely.

Antonio.

No, it won't be him; I cannot
Say I saw the horse a-jumping.

Count.

Bah! I'll soon cut short this nonsense.

Countess. Susanna.
(Aside.)

Gracious powers! What now will happen?

Count.

Go on. You—

Figaro.

Jumped out o' window.

Count.

What induced you?

Figaro.

Fright.

Count.

Of what, sir?

Figaro.

Shut up, waiting for my sweetheart,
Crick-crack came a noise unusual;
You cried out; and I, reminded
Of the note, leaped from the casement
And have sprained my foot.
(Rubs his foot. Antonio pulls out some papers.)

Antonio.

These papers,
Then, belong to you; you dropped them.

Count.

Give them to me.
(Antonio gives them.

Figaro.

I'm caught!

Countess. Susanna.
(Aside.)

Be cautious.

Count.

Now, sir, explain. What is this paper?
(Showing Figaro at a distance.)

Figaro.

Wait—I'll tell you—I've so many.
(Pulls out a lot of memoranda from his pocket
and examines them.)

Antonio.

P'r'aps a list of debts, your lordship.

Figaro.

No, a list of invitations.

Count.
(To Figaro.)

Speak.
(To Antonio.)

You leave him.

Countess and *Susanna.*

Yes, you leave him,
And be off.

Antonio.

I'm going.—Look you
If again I find you skulking—

Figaro.

Go, old fellow, I don't fear you.
(Exit Antonio. The Count again shows the paper;
the Countess recognizes the commission.)

Count.

Come!

Countess.
(Aside to Susanna.)

Oh, heavens! the commission!

Susanna.
(Aside to Figaro.)

Good gracious! the commission!

Count.

Now then!

Figaro.
What a good for nothing
Head is mine!   That!   the commission
Which he had not long since gave me.

Count.
What to do?

-Figaro.
It lacks—

Count.
What lacks it?

Countess.
(Aside.)
Lacks the seal.

Susanna.
(Aside to Figaro.)
The seal—seal tell him.

Figaro.
Why, a seal is mostly added.

Count.
(Aside.)
Oh, this villain will drive me distracted,
Ne'er unriddled the secret will be.
(Twists up the paper.)

Countess.   Susanna.
(Aside.)
If I only escape from this tempest,
I will never tempt further the sea.

Figaro.
(Aside.)
The poor beggar may stamp and may
   bluster,
But he knows less about it than me.
(Enter Bartolo, Marcellina and Basillio.)

Marcellina.   Bartolo.   Basillio.
You, my lord, are famed for justice :
On that justice we rely.

Count.
(Aside.)
These are come, then, to avenge me,
Even now relieved am I.

Countess.   Susanna.   Figaro.
These are come to disconcert us :
To what aid can we apply ?

Figaro.
(To the Count.)
These are lunatics—three idiots .
What can they be after, pray ?

Count.
Softly now, without confusion
Hear what each one has to say.

Marcellina.
(Pointing to Figaro.
This man here has offered marriage,
Promised it me, sir, in writing ;
And I claim that the fulfillment
Of that vow shall now take place.

Countess.   Susanna.
How—why—what !

Count.
Ho there—be silent
I am here to judge the case.

Basillio.
I, a citizen of standing,
Come to offer testimony;
I bear witness to the promise
And to money lent beside.

Countess.   Susanna.   Figaro.
They are lunatics, are raving.

Count.
Silence there !   We'll ascertain it,
We shall read the contract over,
All in order shall be tried.

Countess.   Susanna.   Figaro.
(Aside.)
I'm astounded, I'm bewildered,
Desperate and all confounded.
Certainly some imp of mischief
Sent them on an evil tide.

Count.   Marcellina.   Bartolo.   Basillio.
This is capital, 'tis splendid !
Out of joint are all their noses.
Surely some propitious genius
Sent us on a lucky tide.

TRISTAN AND ISOLDE.

RICHARD WAGNER.

PRELUDE AND FINALE.

IN *Tristan and Isolde* Richard Wagner reveals the fullest development of his theory of endless melody. The opera has been heard frequently at the Metropolitan, and the poetic structure from which the composer gained the musical completion of the work is well known to New York audiences. When the Prelude was first produced, over thirty years ago, it left a chaotic impression upon audiences. Wagner showed his own belief in himself characteristically when he determined to give it in Paris, in 1860, to a public for the most part hostile to him, and which later refused, under the lead of the members of the Jockey Club, to accept his *Tannhäuser*. He gave three concerts in the Theatre Italien, and the Tristan overture was received with constantly increasing appreciation, except on the part of Berlioz, who confessed his inability to understand it. "I have read the curious score of this Prelude through again and again" he wrote. "I have listened to it with every possible attention, inspired with the greatest desire to be able to grasp its significance. But I have to confess that I have not the slightest idea of what the composer wants to say." Berlioz would doubtless be surprised if he could come to life again to-day to find with what enthusiasm this same Prelude is received in Paris to-day by the Paris public.

In *Tristan*, Wagner has released melody from the bonds of a definite, restricted rhythmical period; given it the form of what he calls infinite or endless melody—melody whose origin is not in dance rhythm, but in the free rhythm of musical expression. The motives of the prelude are consequently of a somewhat fragmentary nature, to a certain extent simply interjections, from which is created by means of skillful thematic development a tone picture of marvelous unity and completeness. Edward Schuré, the noted French Wagnerian, says of the music drama: — "A work of profound passion, fiery and concentrated, born of strong personal emotions, yet moving in a region beyond that of reality. At once the boldest, most audacious, yet spontaneous expression of the genius of Richard Wagner, it is the most moving, the most human of dramas, but transfigured by the double magic of Legend and Music. Tristan and Isolde! These two names, inseparably bound together, call up an era out of the twilight of semi-oblivion. During centuries the story of their love lived on the lips of men. It was transmitted by the Gallic bards to the Anglo-Norman singers, by these to the French troubadours, from whom it passed into all the countries of Europe. If the legend of the Holy Grail represents religious chivalry, the mystic conquest of divine love, the story of Tristan and Isolde represents worldly chivalry in the service of terrestrial love that rules all hearts. Breton bards, minstrels and troubadours vied with each other in singing of the numerous adventures of Tristan, the nephew of King Mark, and of Queen Isolde; of their amours at the court of the King, their retreat and their life in the cave of the giants, of their cruel separation caused by Tristan's exile, of Isolde's journey across the sea in order to rejoin him, and finally of their death, uniting both.

"In *Tristan*, poetry and music, welded together by the might of genius, give expression to the tragedy of love with an energy of passion and a plenitude of sentiment that have never been equaled. The music is endless melody. It is a great advance on *Lohengrin*, where harmonic warp and woof dominate the characters. In *Tristan* the organism of the soul, the incessant working of sentiment and thought are revealed. . . Harmony and melody resemble a deep river of passion, which now rushes on confined between its banks, now dashes and foams upon the rocks, now widens into an immense lake; now precipitates itself over cataracts, finally to be lost, as with Isolde's last song, in the silence and majesty of the ocean. The final impression is that of a great calm after a most violent storm. More clearly than ever is revealed the significance of the lives of the unhappy Leopardi. Born at the same time, Love and Death are brothers; not the world below nor the stars above have anything more beautiful."

The scene of the *Finale* is in the courtyard of Tristan's castle in Brittany, whither the Knight has fled after having been wounded by Melot for treachery to the King in winning the love of the Irish Princess. Isolde has followed him across the sea, and King Mark has hastened to the side of his nephew to give his forgiveness to the love-smitten couple. They arrive too late, for Tristan dies in Isolde's arms after a single word of greeting. Isolde sings her famous lament over Tristan's body:—

(Isolde enters. Tristan, unable to control himself, plunges, totteringly, towards her. They meet. Isolde receives him in her arms.)

Isolde.

Tristan ! Ha !

Tristan.

(Dying, looking up to Isolde.)

Isolde !

(He dies.)

Isolde.

'Tis I ! Isolde !

O my beloved !
Wake up once more !
Hark to my voice !
Hearest thou not ?
—Isolde calls—
—Isolde came
With Tristan truly to die !
Will thou not speak ?
But for one moment
Linger. O lov'd one.

Look to the light !
Such dreary days
I have waited, forsaken,
For this brief hour
With thee, love, to waken !
Betrayed was Isolde ?
Betrayed by Tristan
Of one last, fleeting
Hour of bliss,
In earth's last joyous greeting !
Where are his wounds,
That I may them heal ?
That the Night her wonders,
Her rapture reveal ?
Not on thy wounds—
Not thy wounds—be ended the strife !
But blended in love
Be extinguished the light of our life !—
All broken his look !
Still the heart !
Could Tristan truly
From me thus part ?
Not e'en a gentle
Flutter of breath !
Now she must sorrow,
Looking at death,
Who, so joy'd with thee to be wedded,
Bravely came over the sea !
          *   *   *
(Unconscious of all that has been passing around
her, fixes her gaze with estatic fondness and
inspiration upon Trisan's body.)
Mild and sweetly
See him smiling :
See his eyelids
Softly open !
Look you, comrades,
See ye not !
How in radiant
Light he rises,
Bright and lustrous,
Lov'd and lordly,
Starlight-haloed,
Borne on high,
See ye, comrades ?
See ye not ?
How his heart, in

Rapture stress'd,
Stirs and rises
In his breast !
Through his lips so
Sweet and mild,
Breathes his spirit
Reconcil'd :—
Comrades, see—
See and hear ye not ?
To me only
Do they render
All their songs in
Accents tender,—
Sorrow-burden'd,
Rapture-guerdon'd,
Softly moaning,
All-atoning,
Upward soaring,
In me pouring,
Echoing round me,
Love imploring !
Louder sounding,
Me surrounding;
Sound that through the
World rejoices,
Waves of wondrous
Yearning voices,
Tones that swell and
Sink and darken,—
Shall I breathe them,
Shall I hearken ?
Shall I sip them,
Dive within them ?
Leaving life and
Yearning in them ?
In the billowy surge,
In the echoing dirge,
In the wildering world-breath
Joyously merge,
And in desiring
Sweet expiring,—
As in a dream,
Find rapture supreme !

(Isolde sinks, as if transfigured, in Brangaene's
arms, softly upon Tristan's body. Deep emotion and sorrow among those standing around.
King Mark invokes a blessing upon the dead.
The curtain falls slowly.)

(John P. Jackson's Translation.)

ARIA

FROM

"LE ROI DE LAHORE," - - MASSENET.

Promesse de mon Avenir.

UX troupes du Sultan qui menacient Lahore,
    La royale cité,
    Notre puissance est redoutable encore.
Comme si les chassait une invisible main,
Elles ont du désert regagné le chemin.
  Le peuple est rassuré
  C'est mon nom qu'il acclame,
  Le calme est rentré dans mon âme
    Et je puis être heureux !

      Promesse de mon avenir,
      O Sitâ, rêve de ma vie!
      O beauté qui me fus ravie,
      Enfin tu vas m'appartenir.

O Sitâ !—Viens charmer mon cœur amoureux,
  Viens sourire aux splendeurs du monde,
Viens charmer mon cœur amoureux !
  O Sitâ, viens, je t'attends, je t'aime !
  Ma main te garde un diadéme.

      O Sitâ, viens, je t'attends!—
      O Sitâ, viens, je t'attends!! je t'aime !
      Sitâ, tu seras reine !

Ah ! viens charmer mon cœur amoureux,
Viens sourire aux splendeurs du monde,
    O Sitâ, rêve de ma vie,
Viens charmer mon cœur amoureux,
    Viens ! Sitâ, ah, viens !

The Seven Words

OF OUR DEAR REDEEMER AND SAVIOUR
The Lord Jesus Christ SPOKEN BY HIM
AS HE HUNG ON THE SACRED TREE.

✠

TOUCHINGLY SET TO MUSIC BY HEINRICH SCHÜTZ, KAPELLMEISTER AT CASSEL.
(1585=1672.)

FOR FIVE SOLO VOICES, CHORUS, STRING ORCHESTRA AND ORGAN.

✠

In living for the world, thou'rt dead
And sorrow Christ receiveth.

But an thou diest in HIS wounds so red,
Within thy heart HE liveth.

✠

HEINRICH SCHÜTZ' *The Seven Words* is now heard for the first time in America. It is a work of peculiar interest in the history of religious music in general, occupying a place half-way between the music which accompanied the Mysteries and Miracle plays of the thirteenth and fourteenth centuries and the Oratorio as we know it from Handel's day to the present time. The old Passion-plays, to which we trace the modern musical drama, lasted well into the Middle Ages, and in Luther's day they were still a feature of religious life. The best known of those still left to the world, with the original traditions and religious spirit clinging to it, is that given every ten years in the little village of Ober-Ammergau, in the Bavarian Highlands.

In the course of time these mysteries and passion-plays deteriorated so much into buffoonery that they were finally prohibited by the authorities, and by the church itself, and religious musical dramas given under the superintendence of the clergy took their place. San Pleppo Neri, who was born at Florence in 1515, and is famous as the founder of the Congregation of the Oratory, began the dramatization and performance of biblical stories, such as *The Good Samaritan, The Prodigal Son* and *Tobias and his Angels*, accompanied with music, written by Giovanni Animuccia. The term Oratorio became the accepted title for this class of work. Gradually, with the Reformation in Germany, came the musical compositions illustrative of the passion of Christ, which form the connecting link between the works of the Italian composers already mentioned and the oratorio as it developed under Handel.

The earliest forms are found in the *Passio secundum Matthæum* by Stephani, a Nuremberg composer of the sixteenth century, but Schütz was the first to establish the passion-music in genuine oratorio form. He was born in 1585 and died in 1672. Gifted with a beautiful voice, he gained a position in the court-chapel of the Landgrave Moritz of Hesse-Cassel, well known as the writer of many meritorious church compositions. This prince sent the young singer to study for a period of four years with the famous Gabrielli of Venice. Returning to Germany, he was from 1613 to 1615 the Landgrave's court-organist, and from that time until his death he held the position of Electoral Saxon Kapellmeister in Dresden.

Retaining his native German force and solidity, Schütz gave to his works the beauty of Italian form. He left six oratorio-compositions, namely, *The Resurrection of Christ*, which was first performed in Dresden in 1623, and which is regarded as the foundation of German oratorio ; *The Seven Words of Christ*, which was written some time about the year 1645, and four works on the *Passion of Our Lord*, according to the Evangelists (Matthew, Mark, Luke and John), which date from the year 1665. All these show great progress from the earlier works on the Passion.

The editor of the German edition of *The Seven Words*, Carl Riedel, says:— "Interesting as is Schütz' work in its historical relation, a careful and loving study and an exact understanding of it will imbue musicians and dilettantes with the fullest and highest regard for the most prominent of German composers, produced by the times of the Thirty Years' War. They will be astonished at the lovely form of the work, as well as the deep and truthful German expression of feeling. They will have heartfelt satisfaction with the rendition of this small Passion-oratorio, and always return with gladness to it."

After Schütz' death the next works of importance in the same class were in 1704, Bernhard Kaiser's *The Bleeding and Dying Jesus* and Handel's *Passion nach Cap. 19, S. Johannis*, a weak prelude to that composer's later colossal works. Between 1705 and 1718 Kaiser, Handel, Telemann and Matthison prepared the way for the great oratorios of Carl Heinrich Graun, who gave greater significance to the chorale treatment of oratorio, and Johann Sebastian Bach, the father of modern music, who, in his St. Matthew, reached the sublimest form of the Passion-oratorio.

The Seven Words.

✠

Since Christ our Lord was crucified,
And bore the spear wound in his side,
With pain and anguish cruel,
Keep in your hearts the words He spoke,
Each like a holy jewel.

✠

II.—SYMPHONIA.

III.

Evangelist.

And it was close upon the third hour when they crucified the Lord, and Jesus spake :

Jesus.

Father, forgive them, for they know not what they do.

Evangelist.

There stood by the Cross of Jesus, Mary his mother, Mary his mother's sister, the wife of Cleophas, also Mary Magdalene.

When Jesus therefore saw his mother standing near the Cross, with the one loved, the dearest of His disciples, He spake :

Jesus.

Lo, woman, this is thy son.

Evangelist.

Then to His disciple He saith :

Jesus.

Beloved, this is thy mother. Behold her !

Evangelist.

From that moment forth that disciple took her.

Soprano.

Straightway, one of the malefactors, which had been hanged, railed on Him and said :

The Thief on the Left.

If thou be the Christ, then help thyself and us.

Evangelist.

Eftsoons answered the other, chiding him, and spake :

The Thief on the Right.

Oh thou, hast thou then no fear of God ? Seeing thou the same condemnation hast. Indeed, we are justly condemnèd ; for we receive due reward for deeds we have wrought ;

But, remember, naught amiss hath ever this man done.

Evangelist.

And unto Jesus he said :

The Thief on the Right.

Lord, be mindful of me when Thou to Thy kingdom comest.

Evangelist.

And Jesus said:

Jesus.

Truly J say to thee, thou with me shalt to=day in Paradise be.

The Four Evangelists.

And at about the ninth hour He cried aloud and said:

Jesus.

Eli, Eli, lama sabachthani.

Evangelists.

Which is interpreted:

Jesus.

My God, my God, wherefore hast Thou forsaken me?

Evangelist.

And after this, when Jesus knew that all things were done, that the Word might be fulfillèd, he saith:

Jesus.

J thirst.

Evangelist.

And one among the soldiers present ran in haste, filled a sponge with vinegar and hyssop, and brought it, and put it upon a reed, and to His lips he raised it, and gave Him to drink.

Now when Jesus the vinegar had received He said:

Jesus.

'Tis finished!

Evangelist.

And once again He cried aloud and said:

Jesus.

Father, my spirit J commend into Thy hands.

Evangelists.

And after He had thus spoken He inclined His head and gave up His spirit

———

IV.—SYMPHONIA.

✠

Chorus of the Congregation:

Now ye who honor the woes of God,
And oft recall This seven words;
Will find your God ever present,
Both here on earth, where once He trod,
And there in the light of Heaven.

SULAMITH.

LEOPOLD DAMROSCH.

FOR SOLI, CHORUS AND ORCHESTRA.

THE production of Dr. Leopold Damrosch's *Sulamith* at the present Festival must naturally assume the character of a service in honor and memory of the founder of the Oratorio Society and of the Symphony Society, of New York, both of which have since the father's death, February 15, 1885, been under the leadership of Mr. Walter Damrosch, his son, who has been enabled to see accomplished the plans of which, under less favorable conditions, the father could only dream. Had the father lived he could have exclaimed with Wotan : " Achieved is the wonderful work ; as in my dreams I dreamt it ; such as it was in my will," and contemplated the new home of the two societies and of music in general with more satisfaction than could the old Teutonic god, upon whose Walhalla rested such a fearful mortgage until the flames consumed it and the divinities.

Dr. Leopold Damrosch occupied when he died a proud position in the American musical world, one which he had attained by true, conscientious and unwearying artistic work. He enjoyed a great European reputation before his arrival here, in 1871, at the invitation of the Arion Society, but his best and most enduring work was done after that for the American musical world. The Oratorio and Symphony Societies, and the first season of grand German opera at the Metropolitan, are the monuments which attest that fact.

" For years," said a biographer at the time of Dr. Damrosch's death, " before his musical activity began here the city had practically been without a firmly established and worthy choral organization, except the Liederkranz and Arion, which are German institutions. The large choirs which existed when he came were torn by internal dissensions, and were accomplishing little else than to perpetuate the Christmastide performances of *The Messiah*. Dr. Damrosch had naturally a longing to stand at the head of a capable choral society, but he knew the difficulties

40 *Fourth Concert, Friday Evening.*

in the way of establishing one, and for two years confined his efforts to the narrow and unsatisfactory field afforded him by the Arion, a society of men singers. In the spring of 1873 Mrs. Morris Reno and other friends called upon him and urged him to organize a mixed choir. He consented to take the direction of one, and two weeks afterward the first meeting of the nucleus of the future Oratorio Society was held in Dr. Damrosch's house, which then was in Thirty-fifth street. There were twelve or fifteen men and women present, all of whom pledged themselves to do missionary work for the new enterprise and bring additional voices to the next meeting. Trinity Chapel was secured for a study room, and the work was begun with a zeal equally distributed between the director and his little choir.

"On December 3, 1873, the first concert of the Oratorio Society was given in Knabe's pianoforte warerooms, which had succeeded Trinity Chapel as the place of weekly meeting. The choir by this time numbered fifty or sixty voices. Dr. Damrosch played a violin solo, and took part in some chamber music interspersed with the vocal pieces. The chorus grew steadily. By May 12, 1874, it had not quite one hundred members, but felt itself strong enough to attempt an oratorio with orchestra. Handel's *Samson* was given on that date in Steinway Hall, and the society was launched on its career. For five years Dr. Damrosch gave it his services gratis, but after that it was so well established that it needed no such sacrifice. It now ranks with the foremost choirs of the world. In the twelve years of its existence, up to the time of Dr. Damrosch's death, the Oratorio Society had performed the following large choral works, besides many of lesser moment :

Title.	Composer.	Title.	Composer.
Actus Tragicus	Bach	L'Allegro, Il Pensièroso ed Il Moderato	Handel
St. Matthew Passion	Bach	Israel in Egypt	Handel
Vain and Fleeting	Bach	The Creation	Haydn
Grande Mess deo Mortes	Berlioz	The Seasons	Haydn
German Requiem	Brahms	Christus (two parts)	Kiel
St. Ursula	Cowen	St. Paul	Mendelssohn
Ruth and Naomi	Damrosch	Elijah	Mendelssohn
Sulamith	Damrosch	First Walpurgis Night	Mendelssohn
Scenes from Orpheus	Gluck	Tower of Babel	Rubinstein
The Messiah	Handel	Paradise and the Peri	Schumann
Judas Maccabeus	Handel		
Alexander's Feast	Handel		

"During the first few years of its existence the Oratorio Society co-operated at intervals with Mr. Thomas' orchestra. When this was dissolved, in 1877, Dr. Damrosch and his friends organized the Symphony Society, which afterwards remained under his baton, and worked hand in hand with the choral organization. The two most striking products of this co-operation, under the direction of Dr. Damrosch, were the first performance in this country of Berlioz' *Damnation of Faust*, at a series of concerts in 1879 and 1880, and the Musical Festival of 1881, held in the

Leopold Damrosch: Sulamith. 41

Seventh Regiment Armory. At this festival Rubinstein's *Tower of Babel* and Berlioz' *Requiem* were performed for the first time in America. The chorus numbered 1,200 voices, the orchestra 250 instruments, and in spite of the vast expense incurred by the gathering and drilling of such forces, and the engagement of eminent solo singers, the festival was financially successful."

Dr. Damrosch crowned his great work for music in New York by carrying to a brilliant success what then seemed a very hazardous experiment—that of establishing German Opera at the Metropolitan Opera House. He was the first to give the Wagnerian opera in high, artistic shape. He had just completed the arduous rehearsals, and had given the first performance of Wagner's *Valkyr*, and was dreaming of introducing the later music dramas of the Bayreuth Master the following season, when he fell a victim to overwork, and his death was mourned as a public calamity. The funeral solemnities for the dead leader were held at the Metropolitan Opera House. There was never before such universal appreciation shown by the metropolitan public for the loss of a great benefactor. The funeral eulogies were contained in a beautiful letter by Bishop Potter and an address by the Rev. Henry Ward Beecher.

Dr. Damrosch's life-work was directed to the artistic interpretation of the highest musical ideals. "Art," he said, in his address to the Nineteenth Century Club, in March, 1884, "must be lifted to the position of religion, and religion is dependence and obedience. Equality is a political thing, but it has no place in Art. So long as the world lasts there will be rich and poor. But there is a great charity which we in America can give—that is, education to every one, and especially in Art." Dr. Damrosch was a composer of high attainments. Two of his works, *Ruth and Naomi* and *Sulamith*, appear in the list of those sung by the Oratorio Society. The latter was written for and dedicated to the Society, and had its first production in New York in the year 1882. One of his most successful compositions was his *Festival Overture*, which he wrote in 1865 for the inauguration of the Grand Opera House at Breslau, and which was heard here at the grand Festival in 1881. In 1870 it was given at the festival of the United Musicians of Germany, at Weimar, and Raff, who heard it, volunteered, in testimony of his high appreciation of the work, to make a pianoforte arrangement of it for four hands, which he did. On November 23, 1884, his Violin Concerto was played at the Symphony Society's Concert, by M. Ovid Musin.

In dying, Dr. Damrosch was sustained by the thought that beyond his work accomplished he left hostages to the perpetuation of his name and the pursuance of his high endeavors. His last words were to leave the legacy of his work to be completed by his son. He was assured that all would go well, and then, in disjointed phrases, he asked that the great work he had commenced should go on as if he were in life, and then, calm and composed, undisturbed by the prospect of death, he breathed his last. Such a life could not, indeed, end with death. It lives on in his teachings and in the heritage he left to those imbued so thoroughly with the spirit that inspired him. The music world acknowledges, for the father's sake, the son, whose education and training fitted him to carry out his father's ideas. To this end he needed the artistic devotion of those whom his father gathered around him, and this was given him, and the result is seen in the splendid Music Hall, now inaugurated as the home of the two societies which he founded.

Brought up in an atmosphere of music, benefited by the instruction of his father, Walter Damrosch became an accomplished musician at an early age. At the age of nineteen he came prominently before the public as conductor of the Newark Harmonic Society. Under his direction this Society produced Beethoven's *Choral Fantaisie*, Rubinstein's *Tower of Babel*, and other pieces of an equally high order. When Dr. Damrosch conducted the great musical festival at the Seventh Regiment Armory in 1881 his son officiated as assistant, through weeks of arduous rehearsals. After his father's death, in 1885, he was called upon to conduct the Metropolitan Opera season to its close. He stood the ordeal of carrying that work through so successfully that he was appointed the leader of the opera for a supplementary tour that season, and the following year was made the Assistant to the Director, and shared with him the duty of selecting in Germany the singers for the following season, many of whom have won fame while with us.

He was also chosen as the successor to his father as the leader of the Oratorio and Symphony Societies, after due deliberation and trial. Predisposed toward him, on his father's account, they nevertheless felt that the standard of performances must continue lofty. His term of trial was to last through the unfinished season of four concerts. All concerned understood that if he should not meet the requirements another conductor would be found for the ensuing season. At all hazards, the interests of the Societies were to be of prime consideration. The first concert under this arrangement went far to quiet apprehensions that the new conductor's work might be disappointing. At the second concert these fears were entirely overcome. The remaining two concerts made the triumph complete, and Walter Damrosch was regularly and unconditionally installed as the conductor of the Oratorio and Symphony Societies.

The public is reasonably informed about what the Oratorio and Symphony Societies have done under him. They have produced the great chorals with entire acceptability, and they have done much that was never before attempted by them ; notably, the full oratorio of Liszt's *Christus*, which before had been given only in part ; Berlioz' *Romeo and Juliet*, the *Damnation of Faust* and Grell's *Missa Solemnis*. The last-named work abounds in difficulties so stupendous as to have discouraged its performance ever before in this country. Indeed, it has but rarely been attempted in Europe, for although musicians have known of it for years as a masterly production, singularly effective in its possibilities and constructed with marvelous contrapuntal skill, it stood beyond the reach of all except the most advanced choral societies, and even they fought shy of it.

It happened that Dr. Von Bulow attended the concert at which this work was given. Von Bulow's tongue and pen are not easily tempted to praise. The value and correctness of his judgment are held in the highest esteem. The performance led him to write to Mr. Damrosch. His estimate may be sufficient to show how a very great musical authority regarded the work of the conductor of the present Festival:—

MY DEAR FRIEND AND VALIANT YOUNG COLLEAGUE : You gave me last night a very, very great pleasure, such as has seldom been afforded me ; and you know how genuinely happy I am when I am able to admire sincerely an artistic performance. This was the case last night. Your chorus is a "collective virtuoso," such as the oldest and most celebrated institutions of the kind in the German Emperor's city of Berlin cannot hope to approach. How happy would the departed author of the wonderful art-work have been if he could have been present at its transatlantic interpretation ! "Per aspera ad astra ! " I exclaimed again and again while the intoxicatingly beautiful sounds of so many well-schooled throats came to my ears. If the spirit of my old and revered comrade, Leopold Damrosch, could only have listened to the endeavors of the son, the worthy successor and continuer of the work begun by him ; the artistification of the land of freedom ! But he does continue to live in you. "Macte virtute tua Valteri ! Vale et me ama ! "

SULAMITH.

No. 1. *Prelude.—Orchestra.*

No. 2. *Duet for Soprano and Tenor.*

Tell me, O thou whom my soul loveth, where thou feedest, where thou makest thy flock to rest at noon.

No. 3. *Tenor Solo with Male Chorus.*

Behold, thou art fair, my love ; thou hast dove's eyes. Thou art the rose of Sharon and the lily of the valley. As the lily among thorns, so is my love among the daughters.

No. 4. *Mixed Chorus.*

Arise, my love, my fair one, and come away. For lo, the winter is past, the rain is over and gone ; the flowers appear on the earth ; the time of the singing of birds is come, the voice of the turtle is heard in our land. Arise, my love, my fair one, and come away.

No. 5. *Soprano Solo.*

I rose to unlock for my beloved, with sweet fragrant myrrh perfumed the limbs : I longed for my beloved in the night, I waited in vain—and I fell asleep: —Hark ! it knocketh, hark ! the dearest voice sounds forth ! "Oh ! unlock, my love, my dearest sister ! My tender dove, my angel undefiled ! Tarry not, unlock, my love, my angel, unlock !—

Trembling for joy, breathless with rapture, enchanted by his voice, how beats my heart with pulses longing for coming pleasures ! I haste, draw the bolt quickly back—and gaze with terror into the vacant night !—Lo ! I awake and see, it is a dream, a painful dream !—

O, I charge you, daughters of Jerusalem, whene'er you meet my friend : tell him that I am sick with love's desire, tell my sorrows, the griefs of my tortured soul. Conjure him, as I conjure you : to haste, to come and kiss me sound again !

No. 6.   Orchestra.

He brought me to the banqueting house, and his banner over me was love.

No. 7.   Tenor Solo.

"How fair is thy love, my sister, my spouse ; thou hast ravished my heart with thine eyes, with the chain of thy neck. A garden inclosed is my sister ; a spring shut up, a fountain sealed, a fountain of gardens, a well of living waters, and streams from Lebanon."

No. 8.   Octet for Female Voices, without accompaniment.

Whither is thy beloved gone, O thou fairest among women ? Whither is thy beloved turned aside ? that we may seek with thee.

No. 9.   Duet for Soprano and Tenor.

Come, my beloved, let us go forth into the field : let us lodge in the villages. Let us get up early to the vineyards ; let us see if the vine flourish, whether the tender grape appear and the pomegranates bud forth : there will I give thee my loves, O my beloved !

No. 10.   Final Chorus.

Love is strong as death ; many waters cannot quench love, neither can the floods drown it. Love is strong as death.

Beethoven's Fifth Symphony.

C MINOR.

1. ALLEGRO CON BRIO.   3. ALLEGRO, FOLLOWED BY
2. ANDANTE CON MOTO.   4. ALLEGRO (FINALE).

BEETHOVEN'S Fifth Symphony, in C minor, is probably the one most strongly associated with its composer in the mind of the general public. With the rugged strength of this great work, its impassioned violence and the glowing blaze of its color the average listener is more impressed than by the depth of the Ninth, or even the exalted beauty of the Eroica. Its place is in that supreme vantage ground of the composer's life, the second period of his musical evolution. He had shaken free from the trammeling influence of all other creative minds and formal "rule," and was then walking alone over new fields and pastures green in the unexplored realms of music's world.

This new world's wonders required a new language for their description, and the new language was forthcoming in that mighty series of revelations, the nine symphonies. It glowed, perhaps, with a more vivid intensity and passionate brilliancy in the C minor than anywhere else. Certainly it is here that one finds its most startling phase. It is small wonder that in the dazzling brightness of these immortal nine compositions, which seem to have sounded the entire gamut of human feeling, the claim has gone forth that Beethoven has "said the last word" for the symphony. Certainly the force of the word spoken in this Fifth is so mighty that its sound will go rolling down the years to come, as it has in the past, and no future light will ever detract from its power or shadow its glory.

The C minor Symphony is the 67th in number of its composer's works, and until 1813 was known as the 6th, while the Pastoral was called the 5th. The researches of Nottebohm prove that the two symphonies reached their completion during the years 1807 and 1808. Studies for the first movement of the C minor were made some seven years earlier. There is small doubt that the latter takes precedence of the Pastoral in point of time. For although the original manuscript is unnumbered, and is simply inscribed "Sinfonie da L. v. Beethoven," the Pastoral is numbered the 6th in the composer's own hand. The two were brought out together at a concert in the "Theater an der Wien," December 22d, 1808.

I. ALLEGRO CON BRIO.—Of the simple opening theme on which the *Allegro con brio* is built, a theme consisting of only two notes, Beethoven himself is reported to have said:—"So pocht das Schicksal an die Pforte" (Thus fate knocks at the portals). It is from this simple subject, however, that the master-hand created an opening movement so wild, impetuous and stormy that when Goethe, who was in nowise predisposed to favor Beethoven's music, first heard it he exclaimed:—"It is very grand, wildly mad. It makes one fear that the house is about to fall down." It has been suggested that the actual notes of this subject were possibly those of some bird's call. If this be so it was veritably a cry that proved the "open sesame" to a mystic realm. At the feeble call from a bird's tiny throat open flies the sealed portal which leads into the uttermost depths of human nature, stormy and tempestuous, assailed by direst foes, encompassed by a darkly overshadowing fate, and well nigh overwhelmed by its vain struggles. Beethoven in this first movement sets forth a human soul struggling against its own bitterness.

In this symphony above all others the searcher after the meaning and portent of this vague language of music seeks not for an explanation of its mysteries in any set picture, nor tries to express it in any form of words. He looks for its meaning into his own soul, and finds it there according to his own measure of the heights and depths of humanity. But two subjects enter into the composition of the *Allegro*—the one already mentioned and the counter-theme, an almost equally simple one, of eight notes, introduced by the horn and then taken up successively by violins, clarinet and oboe. Out of these two short subjects the entire movement, in all its intricacy, is evolved. No new matter is introduced as groundwork for the tale of heavy human misery the teller is unfolding, nor to help out the variety of incident, yet the treatment of this small field, although of the strictest and most concise, presents with all the force of vividest picturing the intensest emotion capable of expression.

Berlioz says of this movement :—"It (the first) is devoted to a delineation of boundless feelings which agitate great souls and bring them to the verge of desperation. Not that quiet, submissive hopelessness which has the appearance of resignation, nor the mute and gloomy sorrow of a Romeo when he hears of the death of his Juliet, but the rage of a terrible Othello while he listens to those venomous calumniations from the mouth of Iago which convince him of the guilt of Desdemona. Now it is the frenzied rage of insanity, which finds expression in fearful cries, and anon utter despondency, which speaks only in tones of longing sadness and self-commiseraton. Mark the sobbing in the orchestra, the dialogue between the wind and string instruments, whose sounds, decreasing in power, ebb and flow like the stertorous breathing of a dying man, but only in a moment to give place to a more intense thought, which kindles the orchestra into a new blaze of rage. Mark the trembling manner as they hesitate for a moment, then suddenly break forth in all their overwhelming power, like a double stream of lava, divided into two kindling unisons, and say if this passionate style does not surpass everything yet achieved in instrumental music."

II. ANDANTE CON MOTO.—The second movement, *Andante con moto*, is in the key of A flat. Here the mood has changed and softened. It is still sad, with a beautiful grace of sorrow, but it has become tender, daintily poetical, even joyful at times, as though the soul whose conflicts the opening portrays had passed into calmer and more hopeful state, and although even yet disturbed by passing doubts and fears looked forward to a triumphant emancipation from its dark dreams and to final victory. The whole movement is worked out on three themes of exquisite beauty, and with a marvelous variety and unsurpassed grace of treatment. On the last repetition of the second of these Beethoven, by a slight alteration of the notes, a trifling extension of the phrase and a management of *nuance* all his own, has produced one of the most pathetic and beautiful effects possible. Immediately after which touching farewell, as if ashamed of being seen with the tears on his cheeks, he urges the basses into *crescendo arpeggio*, and ends the movement with a loud crash and ordinary cadence.

But if Beethoven limited his subjects for the actual treatment of this *Andante* to three only, he permitted to himself during the course of its construction "diversions"—small recreations, as it were, ever and anon interrupting himself in the serious course of progression to throw in a little musical exclamation, or comment, in the most unexpected and bewildering manner. Nowhere is this tendency to "do what he liked" more forcibly exemplified than in one place in this *Andante* where the graceful and even flow of the melody is suddenly suspended, while a rollicking little measure scurries in, conducts itself with much levity through eight bars, and as suddenly disappears, as the original form, recovering breath from the unceremonious interruption, hastens to take up its rightful place again.

III. SCHERZO.—The *Scherzo* passes at once into the (IV.) *Finale*, as the subject matter, being the same, will not allow of interruption. Of these Berlioz says :—" The *Scherzo* is an extraordinary composition ; the very opening—though containing nothing terrible in itself—produces the same inexplicable emotion that is caused by the gaze of a magnetizer. A somber, mysterious light pervades it ; the play of the instruments has something sinister about it, and seems to spring from the same state of mind which conceived the scene on the Blocksberg in *Faust*. A few bars only are forte-piano, and *pianissimo* predominate throughout. The middle of the movement (the 'trio') is founded on a rapid passage for the double basses, *fortissimo*, which shakes the orchestra to its foundation," retiring by degrees until it is gradually lost. M. Berlioz' analysis continues :—" The theme of the *Scherzo* reappears, *pizzicato*, the sound diminishing at the same time until nothing is heard but the crisp chords of the violins and the droll effect of the upper A flat in the bassoon's rubbing against the G, the fundamental note of the dominant minor ninth. At length the violins subside onto the chord of A flat, which they hold *pianissimo*.

The drums alone have the rhythm of the subject, held with all possible ligntness, while the rest of the orchestra maintains its stagnation.

"The drums sound C, since C minor being the key of the movement : but the chord of A flat, so long held by the strings, forces another tonality on the ear, and we are thus kept in doubt between the two. But the drums increase in force, still obstinately keeping up both note and rhythm; the fiddles have by degrees also fallen into the rhythm, and at length arrive at the chord of the seventh on the dominant (G), the drums still adhering to their C. At this point the whole orchestra —including the three trombones, hithero silent—bursts like a thunderclap into C major, and into the triumphal march which forms the commencement of the *Finale*, the thunder-like effect of which we all know."

Sir George Grove, from whose analysis the above is for the main part taken, says :—" The effect of this transition is obvious enough to the ear, though it may be difficult to explain it to the reader. With reference to it, it is sometimes said that Beethoven has, after all, only made use of the common expedient of following a soft passage in the minor by a burst in the major; that the theme of the *Finale* is not original ; and that the interest of the movement diminishes instead of increasing as it goes on. To which answer may be made that it is no reflection on the genius of a composer that the means he employs are those already in use. Plenty of other composers have used the same expedients, but nothing that they have done can be compared for a moment to this stupendous pæan of victory, in which the soul of Beethoven, for the moment freed from its mortal drawbacks and sufferings, seems to mount to heaven in a chariot of fire. The four first bars of the subject may not be strikingly original, but the forms of the triumphant *fanfare* are but limited, and it is probably not possible to find new ones without forfeiting the simple, grandiose, pompous character which is native to that kind of phrase.

"But Beethoven evidently did not intend to continue the *fanfare* style after the first few bars, and in the rest of the movement he quickly resumes the lofty and original style which never forsakes him. As to the interest not increasing as it goes on, the transition from the *Scherzo* to the *Finale* is probably the greatest effort of which music is at present capable, so that it would be simply impossible to have continued to increase it. And those who thus carp at one of the greatest works of human genius forget what a peculiar charm is given to the movement by the sudden reintroduction of the trio into the midst of it, an expedient most original and producing an effect which has probably never been surpassed.

"It was indeed a prodigious effort even to sustain so lofty a flight; but Beethoven has done it, notwithstanding the extent to which he has developed his subjects."

WAGNER'S PARSIFAL.

PRELUDE AND FLOWER MAIDEN SCENE—ACT II.

FOR SIX SOLO VOICES AND FEMALE CHORUS.

THIS scene is the temptation of Parsifal, the hero of Wagner's last music-drama Parsifal became ruler of the legendary realm of the Grail, after passing through many trials and temptations. Titurel had ruled four hundred years over the Grail kingdom ere he was called to his eternal rest. He was succeeded by his son Frimutelle, who, however, fell from grace. He in his turn was succeeded by Amfortas, who had fallen from his high estate and been wounded in an encounter with Klingsor. The latter had himself once been a Knight of the Grail, but he had been expelled from the order for his sins. He had then built a castle near to Monsalvat and had filled it with beautiful maidens to allure the Knights.

Amfortas had fallen to the wiles of Kundry (Orgeleuse). Klingsor had obtained possession of the Sacred Spear, and hoped in time to possess himself of the Grail. Amfortas, however, was still kept in life by being permitted to look upon the radiance of the Grail. But his wound would not heal; yet the prophecy was that there should come to the Grailburg in good time a pure, youthful knight, who, after passing triumphantly through temptation and mockery, should bring him healing and redemption by touching his wound with the Sacred Lance, but should succeed him as a ruler of the Grail realm. To prevent Parsifal attaining the glories of the Grail, Klingsor has bidden Kundry to call her enchantresses to her assistance and to bring about his downfall. The scene in the opera is a magic garden, with tropical vegetation and most luxuriant growth of flowers. At the back the scene is closed in by the battlements of the castle walls, on which stands Parsifal, gazing down upon the garden in astonishment. From every side, from the garden as well as from the palace, rush in, first singly then in greater numbers, beautiful girls, in garb hastily thrown about them, as if they had been suddenly wakened by fright:—

49

THE FLOWER MAIDENS.

Girls.

Here was the tumult!
Weapons! Wild confusion!

Others.

Horror! Vengeance! Up!
Where is the culprit?

Several.

My belovèd is wounded.

Others.

Pray tell me where mine is.

Others.

I awoke all alone,—
Where hath he vanished?

Still Others.

There in the castle?—
They're bleeding, wounded!
Where is the wretch?
Behold him! Look!
There with my Ferris' sword!
I saw him storm up the walls,
I heard, too, the master's voice,
My knight hastened here;—
They all rushed at him, but each
Was received by his terrible blade.
The fearless! The slaughterer!
All of them fled from him!—
Thou there! Thou there!
Why bring us such direful woe?
Accurst, accurst thou shalt be!

(Parsifal springs down lower to the garden.)

The Girls.

Ha! Stripling! Wouldst thou defy us?
Why hast thou slaughtered our lovers?

Parsifal.

(In great astonishment.)

Ye winsome women—how could I help it?
To such loveliness did they bar me not the
   way?

Girls.

To us wouldst thou come?
Nor saw'st us before?

Parsifal.

Ne'er saw before such lovely delight!
I call ye lovely;—am I not right?

The Girls.

And surely thou wouldst not beat us?

Parsifal.

Nay, surely not.

Girls.

But harm
Full much thou hast done us and griev-
   ous:—
Of our playmates wouldst thou bereave us?
Who'll play with us now?

Parsifal.

Forsooth will I!—

The Girls.

If thou art kind, so pray come nigh—
And then, wilt thou not scold us,
For sweet reward mayst hold us;
For gold we do not play,
Love's gentle meed is the pay;
Wouldst thou comfort us truly,
The winnings earn from us duly?

(Some of the girls have entered the bowers; they
now return, clad in garments of flowers and even
appearing like flowers, and surround Parsifal.)

Flower Maidens.

Hands off the stripling! He belongs to me!
No!—No!—Me!—Me!—

Others.

Oh, the hussies! A trick they've play'd us!

(They retire and return in similar flowery garb.)

The Girls.

Come! Come! Gentle stripling:
I'll be thy blossom;
And in rapturous rippling
Let my love pierce to thy bosom!

(While in graceful play they dance round Parsifal.)

Parsifal.

(Enjoying the scene; standing in their midst.)

How fragrant! How sweet!
Are ye all flowers?

The Girls.

(Sometimes singly, sometimes together.)

The garden's pride,
Whose fragrance and splendor
To the Master in Spring we surrender;

Each bloom a bride,
In sunshine and summer,
Awaiting the call of the comer.
Be to us kind and true,
Nor hoard from the flowers their due!—
And canst thou not love us nor cherish,
Then surely we wither and perish!

Girls.

1. Upon thy bosom let me rest!
2. O Love, let me caress thee!
3. To me let me press thee!
4. I'll close thy mouth with kisses!
5. Nay, I am fairest and best!
6. To me, wouldst know what bliss is!

Parsifal.
(Softly repelling their advances.)
Ye wild, winsome pressure of roses—
If I'm to play with you, your circle too
close is!

Girls.
Surely not wroth?

Parsifal.
I would not harm you!

Girls.
We're quarreling for thee.

Parsifal.
Pray calm you!

First Girl.
Away with you! See, he wants me!

Second.
No, me!

Third.
He mine is!

Fourth.
No, mine!

First (to Parsifal).
Wouldst spurn me?

Second.
Wouldst drive me away?

First.
Art of women so frightened?

Second.
Of fear be thou lightened!

Some.
How cold he is—so bashful in wooing!

Others.
Should flowers, like the bees,
Do all the cooing?

First Half Chorus.
A fool he is surely!

A Girl.
I'm not sad to lose him!

Others.
Then we others will choose him.

Others.
No, we! No, we!—
Me too!—Here! Here!

Parsifal.
(Half in anger turns away, as if to escape.)
Away!—Your wiles are vain!
From a flowery arbor is heard the voice of
Kundry.
Parsifal!—Tarry!—
(The girls are terrified and cease their witcheries.
Parsifal stands dumbfounded.)

Parsifal.
Parsifal . . . —
So once in dreams—I was named by my
mother!

Kundry's Voice.
Nay linger! Parsifal!--
For here shall rapturous bliss be thine!
Ye childish enchantresses, leave him alone:
Flowers, born but to wither:
Not sent was he here for your delight!
Go home, care for the wounded,
Lonely awaits you many a knight.

The Girls.
(Reluctantly leaving Parsifal.)
O the sorrow! this parting grievous!
Alas! Alack a day!
Let all the world beside but leave us,
If he could with us stay.—
Farewell! Farewell!
So gentle! So handsome!
Thou—Fool!

(With the last word they all rush towards the
castle, laughing. Parsifal looks timidly towards
the side whence came the voice. There stands
revealed, through the withdrawal of the branches
of the thicket, a youthful female figure of sur-
passing beauty—Kundry, in her form completely
changed—lying upon a bed of flowers, and clad
in fantastic drapery that lightly veils her form.)

Parsifal passes safely through the ordeal, is found and recognized by Gurnemanz as the promised savior of Amfortas, and by him taken on a Good Friday morning to the realm and castle of the Grail, where he touches the wound of the suffering monarch and is himself made King of Monsalvat. The poem of *Parsifal* was completed by Wagner in the summer of 1877, a year after the first Nibelung Festal Performances at Bayreuth. The musical composition of the work was finished at Palermo, and in July and August, 1882, sixteen performances of the work were given at Bayreuth. On February 13th of the following year the great composer died at Venice. The germ of the *Parsifal* music-drama was born in Wagner's mind much earlier than 1877. The first portions were the " Abendmahl " scene and the "Good Friday Magic." The latter is thought to date from the year 1857. Prof. Tappert says: " Wagner told me (in 1877) that in the fifties when in Zurich he took possession on a Good Friday of a charming new house, and that inspired by the beautiful spring weather he wrote out the sketch that very day of the Good Friday music," the words to which are filled with the highest religious fervor, and which may be quoted as forming a contrast to the wild revelries of the Klingsor flower garden scene :—

Parsifal.

(Turns round and gazes enraptured upon forest and meadow, bathed in the morning light.)

Methinks, to-day the meads are won-
    drous fair !—
Full many a magic flower I've seen
That round my neck all wantonly
    would cluster :
Yet never saw, so mild and sweet,
The frondage, flowers and blossoms,—
Their fragrance pure as child's delight,
And speaking fondest trust to me.

Gurnemanz.

'Tis all Good Friday's magic, Lord !

Parsifal.

Alas! His day of agony!
When surely all that buds and blooms,
And breathing lives, and lives again,
    Should mourn and weep and sorrow.

Gurnemanz.

Thou seest—that is not so—
But sinners' tears it is of penance
That here, with heavenly dew,
    Fall down on mead and field,
      And make them bloom rejoicing;

Now all His creatures live anew,
    And at the Saviour's trace revealed,
      Their praise and prayers are voicing.
Upon the Cross they can not see Him
    languish,
So up to Man Redeemed they, trusting,
    look,
Who feels releas'd from stress of sin and
    anguish,
Through God's great sacrifice made clean
    and pure:
The Flowers well know how love can
    hatred vanquish,
To-day of human feet they have no
    dread:
For as the Lord, with heavenly patience
    filled,
Compassion took and for Men bled,
Now Man to-day, with glory thrill'd,
    Spares them with careful tread:—
    All Creatures that rejoice in life,
    And all that blooms and passes hence,
    See Nature, freed from sin and strife,
    Wake to her day of Innocence.

(Kundry has slowly raised her head and looks with moistened eyes, pleadingly, upon Parsifal.)

Israel in Egypt

(ORATORIO)

FOR SOLI, DOUBLE CHORUS AND ORCHESTRA.

HANDEL.

HANDEL wrote *Israel in Egypt* four years before his *Messiah*. It is the fifth of the nineteen oratorios he wrote for England. It dates from 1738, and was first produced April 4, 1739, at the King's Theatre, of which Handel was then manager. He made several alterations and additions to the score before the work was given a second time, on April 11, and for its third performance, on April 17, a "Funeral Anthem" which he had written for Queen Caroline was used, under the title of "Lamentations of the Israelites for the Death of Joseph." Compared with *The Messiah*, *Israel in Egypt* shows astonishing absence of symmetry. The work was given in mutilated form up till the year 1849, when the Sacred Harmonic Society gave it as it was originally written, and as it is now known, without the funeral anthem or any of the added songs. The edition of the vocal score used at the festival is that edited for the Handel Society of London in 1844 by Mendelssohn, who undertook the task with a fitting reverence for the sanctity of Handel's intentions. The following description of the work is by Mr. Chorley : —

The opening of the Part I. is abrupt, and, though twice written by Handel, gives a poor preface to the splendors within. There is no Overture: merely six bars of recitative for tenor, to introduce the first double chorus. This latter is prepared for by the eight bars of a single contralto voice delivering the theme with a wondrously deep pathos. Strength is given to the close of the phrase—"And their cry came up unto God "—by the use of the mass of treble voices in unison with the altos—this being rendered necessary to balance the muscular phrase in the bass instruments, on the working of which to the words, " They oppressed them with burdens," against the sustained wail or chant, this magnificent chorus in eight parts depends.—It is admirable to see how the two contradictory elements of prisoners and their task-masters—of " cry " and " oppression "—are here at once combined and kept distinct at the close of the movement, where all the eight voices unite to tell how the " Cry come up unto God "—the God who has never forsaken in their distress them that have called on His name. From this point to the end of the work only signs and wonders are vouchsafed in answer to "the cry" for the humiliation of the tyrant, and afterwards thanksgivings for the marvels wrought by the Most High for His chosen people.

After a few bars of tenor recitative—like all the recitatives in this oratorio, of great boldness and vigor—the remainder of the one act (one song excepted) is a chain of choruses. First—The Plague of the Water turned into Blood, and the loathing of the Egyptians to drink of the river—a chorus based on one of the most obvious subjects for a chromatic fugue in being; which has been, again and again, employed and wrought out. Nevertheless, so admirably does the phrase fit the humor of disgust, that it is difficult, for a moment, to recollect how well such phrase is known or not to conceive it invented with an express reference to the portent. The loathing rises to a point of almost intolerable abomination as the close of the chorus draws near. In this plague the consequences of the portent are dwelt on, rather than the miracle itself.

The air which immediately follows ("Their land brought forth frogs") is the first number in which the student may learn to value Handel, by comparing him in description with Haydn. The words suggest associations perilously familiar; but Handel, in place of passing them over rapidly, accepted them with all their consequences. In the chorus which immediately succeeds this air variety had to be given ; and here the instinct of inspiration helped out the musician, in a manner little short of miraculous. Handel seized " He spake the word " by way of giving relief and basis to a picture which, if only made up of detail, must of necessity have been frivolous, petty, and confusing. The air is full of insect myriads (listen to the restless, whirling, shrill accompaniment—a flight of gnats—told in sound with amazing reality), but the Retributive Power who called this plague forth is never, for a moment, to be left out of memory. The sonorous force of this phrase—especially when delivered in antiphony, binding the whole movement together, without disturbance to the freest possible play of description in music—makes this chorus of the most remarkable in a most remarkable series.

More familiar are the two next choruses—the Plague of Hailstones and the Plague of Darkness. The fire is leaping, rioting, tormenting lightning. How frequently Handel disregarded all that moderns look to so anxiously—namely, sequence of keys—could be hardly better exemplified than by the fact that from the insect Plague, in B flat major, he moved quietly to C major, by way of enforcing his next effect. The subject of this chorus, again, is said not to be Handel's own ; but how the treatment of it flashes!—there is no other possible verb—how do recitation and picture go hand in hand,—prodigious energy and clearness, without a thought, or stint, or less vivid inspiration, than the idea of " Fire mingled with the hail" which "ran along the ground!"

After the Plague of Fire, the next was of thick Darkness ! Here, aware of the limits of epithets, when admiration is to be repeated, it may be best merely to speak to fact—merely to point out this recitative chorus (for such it is, without key, or ordinance, or formal structure) as being in its incompleteness more vague, and fearful, and oppressive than any stricter rendering of the words might have made it. In comparison to this, how cruel (to a scimitar-sharpness) is the following chorus : " He smote all the first-born of Egypt"; a fugue in which every phrase of the detached accompaniment is a blow—and a blow strong enough to smite down the chief of all the strength of Egypt. There is more of vengeance and destruction than of omnipotent retribution in this chorus. It is fiercely Jewish. There is a touch of Judith, of Jael, of Deborah in it ; no quarter, no delay, no mercy for the enemies of the Most High. It is the chorus of the unflinching, inflexible, commissioned Angels of the Sword !

The next chorus, " But as for His people, He led them forth like sheep," if showing neither the pillar of cloud nor the pillar of fire, is the pillar of confidence, under whose shelter a nation wandering and oppressed may repose in the dry wilderness of desolation which intervenes between bondage and the promised land. The lovely serenity of this movement places it by itself among these choruses of *Israel*. There is something in it of even enjoyment ; a flow of happy—not stagnant— calm, the effect of which is delicious, after the terrors and severities that have gone before it. The chorus which follows, " Egypt was glad," is that which figures note by note in Sir John Hawkins's " History of Music," as a *Canzona* by Kerl, there printed without words. The verification of a coincidence so strange, and so strangely overlooked, only a few years since, may be said to have re-opened the question of Handel's debts and plagiarisms.

What a print of a giant's foot was made by his first step on the Red Sea shore! How stupendous those few chords,—" He | re | bukèd the Red Sea,—and it was drièd up." Even the very break noted betwixt the " He " and the word "rebukèd," possibly accidental, gives a sort of separateness and sublimity to Him who " holdeth the waters in the hollow of his hand "; and the pauses by suspense add power to the opening phrase of the movement which immediately succeeds,—"He | led them through the | deep,"—the stateliest march of a chosen nation, delivered by Omnipotence, ever set in music. Observe, again, how simple is the opposition betwixt the two subjects of this muscular chorus—an ascending scale in slow tempo being wrought against the descending scale allotted to the words, " As through a wilderness," the latter one at four times the speed of the former. The weight of the lower phrase would not have been felt without the flexibility of the upper one.

Animated, however, as this chorus is, it is not rapid ; but what a tremendous scream of positive triumph is to be found in that one which succeeds—triumph over the enemy overwhelmed by the waters, "not one" of whom was left ! Here is a sublime example of Handel's declamatory power and his immense ease and command of color. The surge, the swell, the storm, the sweep of "the old sea," the wall of waters " on the right hand and on the left," and the Jericho breaking down of that wall when the pilgrims to the Land of Promise had passed through, are in this chorus. The return from such wandering could hardly be more dryly, prosaically typified than in the chorus closing the first part of *Israel* ("And Israel saw "), which may or may not be a pure Handel chorus.

The Second Part of the work, or "The Song of Moses" (as it was originally called), is a thanksgiving anthem after the miraculous sea-deliverance of Israel. That this is on a grander scale than *The Messiah* is obvious. Not only, as we have seen, is a double chorus perpetually used, but more solo singers are indispensable. The key-note of the whole composition is struck at once in its opening chorus, "Moses and the children of Israel"; to which, by the way, the words closing the First Part may have been meant to serve as an after-link, howbeit superfluous. After a pompous prelude on the grandest scale, another *semi-vocal* overture, we have the whole majestic words of *Miriam's Song*,—"I will sing unto the Lord," and the musical themes of the chorus, to which *Miriam* answered, exposed, or treated elaborately, by way of commencement.

It is followed by a duet for soprani—by Erba, not by Handel ("The Lord is my Strength and my Song")—though written in a minor key, written in words little less triumphant than the foregoing. In Mendelssohn's incomparable edition of *Israel* it is caressed by an organ part, the beauty of which, had Handel sat at the organ himself, could not have been exceeded. After a few bars of grave chorus, "He is my God" (with a singularly odd phrase—again Erba's—for the tenors of the second choir, on the repetition of the words, "I will prepare him an habitation"), comes the *alla capella* movement, "And I will exalt him."

Next comes the duet for two basses, "The Lord is a Man of War," one among many serious bass duets which has never been outdone in musical force—in its truth to the sentiment of the words and in its vocal effect. The end of this superb duet (which, although written in a formal time of music, is written, like the songs of *The Messiah*, with a wondrous emancipation from musical formality) spreads and widens, not without a touch of the sea-tragedy, on the words, "Also are drowned," and with consummate vocal and declamatory splendor.

After this brilliant duet there is a moment's respite from the jubilation—a moment's picture of the deep, fathomless ocean—in the introduction to the next chorus. The three bars of bass on the same note (F), and the entire form of the phrase on the words,—"The depths have covered them," have a wondrously majestic calm and amplitude. After this picture, flashes out anew the triumph of *Israel*, in the brilliant double chorus,—"Thy right hand, O Lord," with its second phrase accented by the musician with a foreign accent,—"is become glorious."

The next chorus is one of those which are debatable. The subject of the fugue—"Thou sentest forth Thy wrath"—is, for Handel, dry, uninteresting, and barren of agreement with the meaning of the verse. All of the master-hand that it presents is the repetition of the word "stubble," which brings out the one effect of the movement with a certain force. The next chorus (a single one) seems doubly precious in contrast. The undulating phrase with which it commences bears an almost literal resemblance to that with which Mozart accompanied the words,— "Tranquilla sia l'onda," in the well-known terzett, *"Soave"* (Cosi fan tutte). There is, perhaps, more peculiarity than truth in the treatment of the scene ; at least, during its commencement :—a fathomless serenity in the phrase,—"The waters were gathered together," somewhat at variance with the idea of—"the blast of Thy nostrils." But there is an admirable fertility and grandeur in the words,—

"The floods stood upright as an heap, and the depths were congealed." The close is an example of calm, sonorous grandeur of sound.

The next number ("The enemy said, 'I will pursue'") is the only tenor air in the oratorio; one of those *bravuras* to which allusion has been elsewhere made, not Handel's best *bravura*. The following song ("Thou didst blow with Thy wind")— the one air for soprano—often undersung—is, perhaps, the grandest solo in the oratorio. It is a proud, declamatory song, one to be given with a heart haughty rather than thankful; the adoration is to come later in *Miriam's* "Sing ye to the Lord." The next chorus may be passed by those who accept the idea of things debatable, and the fact—now pretty distinctly accepted—that Handel's *Israel* has many things in it which do not belong to Handel.

The duet for contralto and tenor ("Thou in Thy mercy"), also debatable, is suave, almost to the point of being pathetic. The duet is in D minor. The chorus which follows, "The people shall hear," is in E minor, and offers another despotic proof of Handel's disregard of all conventions in the succession of keys. But this very chorus contains a unique example of instant setting-to-rights. After the chorus was completed Handel found that one clause of the verse, "All the inhabitants of Canaan shall melt away," had been overlooked; and that marvelous episode now existing was inserted by him betwixt the words, "sorrow shall take hold on them," and those, "by the greatness of Thy arm." The close of this chorus, with its ascending minor scales, is extraordinarily difficult to sing in tune by a mass of voices.

The air which follows, "Thou shalt bring them in," a delicious *cantabile* for the contralto, is the only glimpse afforded in *Israel* of the Land of Promise—not taken from a Pisgah top, perhaps, but more dreamily and distantly—a prophecy rather than an assurance. And last, after a recitative offering noble scope for declamation, comes the culminating point and close of the Song of Triumph,—the most stupendous ending, it may be asserted, to any musical work in being. There is wonderful unity and variety in the chant, "The Lord shall reign for ever and ever," a few plain notes broken by the intervening voice of *Miriam*, the prophetess. What a use of a few plain notes! first, in unison by the *alti* and tenors; then with all the force of the entire eight-part choir. And what an enhancement of accompaniment! by a simple amplification of the stately march of the instruments, which at first upbore the chant; after this a few bars of recitative; and then the chant afresh, one-half first, given by the solitary soprano voice of *Miriam*, unaccompanied; then chorused; afterward the second half is accompanied; then taken up by chorus and wrought to a close, with the words :—

> "Sing to the Lord, for He hath triumphed gloriously !
> The horse and his rider hath He thrown into the sea !"

Israel in Egypt.

PART I.

Recitative.

Now there arose a new king over Egypt, which knew not Joseph; and he set over Israel task-masters to afflict them with burthens, and they made them serve with rigor.

Double Chorus.

And the Children of Israel sighed by reason of the bondage, and their cry came up unto God. They oppressed them with burthens, and made them serve with rigor; and their cry came up unto God.

Recitative.

Then sent He Moses, His servant, and Aaron whom He had chosen; these shewed His signs among them, and wonders in the land of Ham. He turned their waters into blood.

Chorus.

They loathed to drink of the river. He turned their waters into blood.

Air.

Their land brought forth frogs, yea, even in their king's chambers.

He gave their cattle over to the pestilence; blotches and blains broke forth on man and beast.

Double Chorus.

He spake the word, and there came all manner of flies and lice in all their quarters. He spake; and the locusts came without number, and devoured the fruits of the ground.

Double Chorus.

He gave them hailstones for rain; fire mingled with the hail ran along upon the ground.

Chorus.

He sent a thick darkness over the land, even darkness which might be felt.

Chorus.

He smote all the first-born of Egypt, the chief of all their strength.

Chorus.

But as for His people, He led them forth like sheep; He brought them out with silver and gold; there was not one feeble person among their tribes.

Chorus.

Egypt was glad when they departed, for the fear of them fell upon them.

Double Chorus.

He rebuked the Red Sea, and it was dried up.

Double Chorus.

He led them through the deep as through a wilderness.

Chorus

But the waters overwhelmed their enemies, there was not one of them left.

Double Chorus.

And Israel saw the great work that the Lord did upon the Egyptians; and the people feared the Lord.

Chorus.

And believed the Lord and His servant Moses.

PART II.

Double Chorus.

Moses and the Children of Israel sang this song unto the Lord, and spake, saying :

Double Chorus.

I will sing unto the Lord, for He hath triumphed gloriously ; the horse and his rider hath He thrown into the sea.

Duet.

The Lord is my strength and my song ; He is become my salvation.

Double Chorus.

He is my God, and I will prepare Him a habitation ; my father's God.

Chorus.

And I will exalt him.

Duet.

The Lord is a man of war, Lord is his name ; Pharaoh's chariots and his host hath He cast into the sea ; his chosen captains also are drowned in the Red Sea.

Double Chorus.

The depths have covered them, they sank into the bottom as a stone.

Double Chorus.

Thy right hand, O Lord, is become glorious in power ; Thy right hand, O Lord, hath dashed in pieces the enemy.

Double Chorus.

And in the greatness of Thine excellency Thou has overthrown them that rose up against Thee.

Double Chorus.

Thou sentest forth Thy wrath, which consumed them as stubble.

Chorus.

And with the blast of Thy nostrils the waters were gathered together, the floods stood upright as an heap, and the depths were congealed in the heart of the sea.

Air.

The enemy said, I will pursue, will overtake, I will divide the spoil ; my lust shall be satisfied upon them ; I will draw my sword, my hand shall destroy them.

Air.

Thou didst blow with Thy wind, the sea covered them ; they sank as lead in the mighty waters.

Double Chorus.

Who is like unto Thee, O Lord, among the gods ? Who is like Thee, glorious in holiness, fearful in praises, doing wonders ? Thou stretchedst out Thy right hand.

Double Chorus.

The earth swallowed them.

Duet.

Thou in Thy mercy hast led forth Thy people which Thou hast redeemed; Thou hast guided them in Thy strength unto Thy holy habitation.

Double Chorus.

The people shall hear and be afraid, sorrow shall take hold on them ; all the inhabitants of Canaan shall melt away ; by the greatness of Thy arm, they shall be as still as a stone till Thy people pass over, O Lord, which Thou hast purchased.

Air.

Thou shalt bring them in, and plant them in the mountain of Thine inheritance ; in the place, O Lord, which Thou hast made for Thee to dwell in ; in the sanctuary, O Lord, which Thy hands have established.

Double Chorus.

The Lord shall reign for ever and ever.

Recitative.

For the horse of Pharaoh went in with his chariots and with his horsemen into the sea, and the Lord brought again the waters of the sea upon them ; but the children of Israel went on dry land in the midst of the sea.

Double Chorus.

The Lord shall reign for ever and ever.

Recitative.

And Miriam, the prophetess, the sister of Aaron, took a timbrel in her hand, and all the women went out after her with timbrels and with dances, and Miriam answered them.

Solo and *Double Chorus.*

Sing ye to the Lord, for He hath triumphed gloriously ; the horse and his rider hath He thrown into the sea.

FIFTY-SEVENTH STREET AND SEVENTH AVENUE,

New York.

Besides the principal Auditorium, "MUSIC HALL" comprises Recital Hall, Chamber Music Hall, Large and Small Banquet Halls and Meeting Rooms with Parlours, suitable for Lectures, Readings and Receptions, as well as Chapter and Lodge Rooms, for Secret Organizations.

For Terms apply to the Administration Office of the Company, on the premises.

www.ingramcontent.com/pod-product-compliance
Lightning Source LLC
Chambersburg PA
CBHW021523270326
41930CB00008B/1066